HOW CLIENTS BUY

HOW CLIENTS BUY

A Practical Guide *to* Business Development *for* Consulting *and* Professional Services

TOM McMAKIN
DOUG FLETCHER

WILEY

Cover design: Wiley

Published by John Wiley & Sons, Inc., Hoboken, New Jersey.
Published simultaneously in Canada.

For general information on our other products and services or for technical support, please contact our Customer Care Department within the United States at (800) 762–2974, outside the United States at (317) 572–3993, or fax (317) 572–4002.

Wiley publishes in a variety of print and electronic formats and by print-on-demand. Some material included with standard print versions of this book may not be included in e-books or in print-on-demand. If this book refers to media such as a CD or DVD that is not included in the version you purchased, you may download this material at http://booksupport.wiley.com. For more information about Wiley products, visit www.wiley.com.

Library of Congress Cataloging-in-Publication Data:

Names: McMakin, Tom, author. | Fletcher, Doug, author.
Title: How clients buy : a practical guide to business development for
   consulting and professional services / by Tom McMakin, Doug Fletcher.
Description: Hoboken, New Jersey : John Wiley & Sons, Inc., [2018] | Includes
   bibliographical references and index. |
Identifiers: LCCN 2017057356 (print) | LCCN 2017058946 (ebook) | ISBN
   9781119434726 (pdf) | ISBN 9781119434757 (epub) | ISBN 9781119434702
   (cloth)
Subjects: LCSH: Consultants–Marketing. | Professions–Marketing. | Customer
   relations.
Classification: LCC HD69.C6 (ebook) | LCC HD69.C6 M3975 2018 (print) | DDC
   001–dc23
LC record available at https://lccn.loc.gov/2017057356

Printed in the United States of America

SKY10024526_012821

*Tom dedicates this book to Harry Wallace and
the crew at PIE for their fellowship and inspiration.
Doug dedicates this book to his parents, Wade and
Mary Lutie, for introducing him to the world of books.*

Contents

Contents

The Problem

A Curious Problem

Was that you we saw last Friday night at the Seattle airport?

We would've said "Hi," but you were on the phone.

We were the guys in blue blazers dragging our roller boards over to Ivar's for a plate of oysters and a Pyramid IPA. You might have seen us pounding out thank-you notes on our phones before the late flight home.

Allow us to introduce ourselves.

Doug leads a business development consulting firm and sits on the board of a midsized consulting firm. Before that, he cofounded a technology-enabled consulting firm that specialized in global web survey projects. He got his start as a management consultant at A. T. Kearney, and before that was trained on GE's leadership development program.

Tom also runs a consulting firm that helps the biggest names in professional services grow their businesses—a kind of consultant to consultants. He was in private equity before that, and in his first big gig served as the chief operating officer of Great Harvest Bread Co.

This is all to say we've spent two lifetimes offering clients consulting and professional services. We've scoped projects, delivered outcomes, wined and dined clients, written white papers, presented at conferences, and relentlessly followed up.

The proof? When people ask our kids what we do, the kids don't know.

"They travel a lot," they say.

We've written this book to describe how clients buy consulting and professional services because we think if more people in our industry could get smarter about how expertise meets the opportunity to help, the world would be a better place. We look around and see lots of thorny problems that need solving. We also see lots of smart people ready to help. The challenge facing them both is to connect with each other more efficiently.

Maybe you're an accountant, a lawyer, or an Internet security specialist. Maybe you consult on strategy, human resources, finance, marketing, operations, or procurement. Or you're a freelance designer or marketing expert. You might be part of a large organization, working for the big consultant Bain, the consulting and accounting firm KPMG, or the human resources specialist AON. You might work out of a handsome glass and steel tower in downtown Boston or Chicago. Or you might be just starting out or recently retired, offering procurement, organizational or training advice, working out of your newly converted guest bedroom.

Either way, this book is for you.

Rainmaking

As a consultant or a person working in professional services, all of us know we have to become rainmakers—the people at the top who bring client business into their firms. In most large firms, you have to be successful bringing in new business to be considered for promotion to partner. And, if you're a founder or cofounder in a small to midsized firm, you live and die by the work you bring in to feed your troops.

It's the harsh imperative of consulting and professional services: being smart about something is not enough. You have to know how to engage with potential clients, understand their unique challenges, and scope business. You have to figure out a way to build a bridge from your expertise to those it can most help. You have to make it rain, *or you will die in the desert of commerce*.

The problem is that selling consulting and professional services is hard. Some would say really, really hard.

It's hard because selling consulting and professional services is different from selling shoes. The former is sold on relationships, referrals, and reputation, while the latter is sold on attributes like size, weight, color, style, and performance. It's the difference between an intangible and tangible sale.

Further, despite the importance of becoming an effective rainmaker, we're never taught how to *sell the work we do*. We're trained as lawyers, accountants, web developers, financial analysts, engineers, or architects, how to do the work, but not in how to bring in new clients.

Then, there's the inconvenient fact that in our line of work, *sales* is a dirty word. While researching for this book, we interviewed dozens of rainmaking pros and were struck by how many of them said, "Never say 'sell.'" In fact, they reported that they don't even think about selling. To them, it's counterproductive. Dominic Barton, Global Managing Partner of McKinsey & Co., one of the world's premier strategy consulting firms, put it this way: "If I mentioned sales in our firm, I'd be hauled up in front of our professional ethics board. It's just not the way we think."

On top of that, our consulting niches are becoming more specific as they become more global. A client today is just as likely to be in Singapore as San Francisco. A generation or two ago, golf on Saturday was a good way to meet new clients. In the twenty-first century, methods like these are outdated.

Finally, much of what we think we know about selling—the need to generate leads, prequalify them, then pitch and close prospects—is wholly inappropriate to consulting and professional services. What really matters is your relationship with a would-be client, which is formed and nurtured over a lifetime.

Call it the rainmaker conundrum: we need to do business development or we die, and yet we're hobbled by obstacles that keep us from effectively developing this very same business.

There must be a better way.

Chuck McDonald, a senior attorney practicing in Columbia, South Carolina, puts it this way:

> The one thing they don't teach you in law school is that the most important thing in private practice is how to get clients. You find out fairly early whether you are going to be able to do that which enables you to climb the ladder within a firm structure. If you're not, you're a fungible good. There are what we call "worker bees," but they just don't get the same, frankly, respect within the firm or the same compensation. So, it is a very important component.

And so, it's strange to us that more isn't written about business development in the consulting and professional services trades. A quick Amazon search of books on the topic of leadership generates a staggering 191,348 listings. Yet you can count on one hand the number of books that have been written on becoming an effective rainmaker in the expert services professions.

Consulting and professional services is a $1.7 trillion global industry, with 6.1 million of us in the United States working as consultants or in professional services. As the U.S. economy has shifted from manufacturing to a more knowledge-intensive economy, the consulting and professional services sector has expanded, enjoying growth that outpaces the wider economy. While gross domestic product grew on average 2.2% over the last two years, the consulting and professional services sector grew on average an astonishing 11.5%. That's five times as fast.

It is high time we got smart about how to connect with those we can best serve.

The Promise of How Clients Buy

We will help you understand how clients buy consulting and professional services. This knowledge will increase the number of clients you have and earn you more money. More importantly, it will cause your expertise to find its home, solve more problems, and make the world a better place.

To be clear, this is not a book on the sales funnel, selling techniques, better prospecting, persuasion, closing, or negotiation tactics. Instead we describe the *client's buying decision journey*, knowing that it is this perspective that can give rise to a business development approach based on service and not manipulation.

Qualities You Do Not Need to Benefit from This Book

- **A certain size:** You can work for a 400,000-person global IT services firm or have recently spun out on your own into a sole proprietorship. The principles of empathy for the customer, which are the foundation upon which increased engagement is built, are the same regardless of scale.

- **A particular kind of expertise:** You grow an HR consulting practice the same way you grow security consulting. Business development for law looks strikingly similar to business development for a strategy consultancy.

- **A sales personality:** It's a myth that only outgoing personalities succeed at building the kind of relationships that produce more engagements. In fact, many of the pros we interviewed reported the opposite.

- **A big budget:** When clients buy services, they do so in similar ways. Those patterns are largely uninfluenced by the size of your business development budget. That's because cash buys you reach and yet services are sold on relationships, which are created one person at a time. While there are useful ways to spend money if you have it, supporting clients as they move through their decision-making journey does not require a lot of cash.

- **A growing industry:** High-growth sectors have challenges where outside expertise is required, but so do more stable industries. Ask any bankruptcy attorney or restructuring consultant if work is slow, and they will disabuse you of the idea that only growing companies hire consultants.

- **A hot product set:** If you bring a product-sales sensibility to services sales, you will be tempted by the idea that new is better, that it is easier to sell the latest generation of phone than one built a decade ago. However, buyers of consulting and professional services are skeptical when expertise is packaged as a "new offering." For them, a trusted advisor who solves problems alongside them is more important than something "new."

- **Level of experience:** The fundamental business development challenges that face young professionals hoping to show off their commercial chops and make partner and those confronting an old hand seeking to broaden their influence are the same.

- **A willingness to live on the road:** Visiting would-be clients is a tried-and-true approach to business development, but there is a raft of technology-based and phone-based approaches that are equally effective at engaging and establishing relationships with potential clients.

- **Marketing expertise:** You're a designer or an accountant, a technologist or an engineer. You didn't spend a ton of your time in school taking marketing courses. No worries. Most marketing focuses on how to sell products, and as we will learn, clients buy services differently.

The Breakthrough

For us, the breakthrough in understanding how to best sell professional services was when we realized that those who successfully build their consulting and professional services practices are students of *how clients buy* and work to support that buying journey using very specific strategies and techniques. They aren't focused on sales at all.

These pros tell us there are very specific requirements that must be satisfied before a client pulls a trigger and decides to buy our services, preconditions we call the Seven Elements of How Clients Buy.

- Prospective clients become *aware* of your existence. This might be from an introduction from a friend, an article you wrote, or because they met you at a conference.
- They come to *understand* what you do and how you are unique. They can articulate what you do clearly to others.
- They develop an *interest* in you and your firm. They have goals, set by themselves or others, and they can see how what you do might be useful in their efforts to realize those goals. What you do is relevant.
- They *respect* your work and are filled with confidence that you can help. They look to your track record, to their peers, and to a variety of social clues to determine if you are credible and likely to move the needle on their goals.
- They *trust* you, confident you will have their best interests at heart.
- They have the *ability* to pull the trigger, meaning they are in a position to corral the money and organizational support needed to buy from you.
- They are *ready* to do something. The timing is right inside their organizations, and they have the headspace to manage you.

The Seven Elements of the Client's Decision Journey

Our Method

The advice that we offer in this book around each of these elements comes from three primary sources:

1. Interviews conducted with over two dozen senior professionals working in a wide range of consulting and professional services, including law, accounting, investment banking, commercial real estate, and management consulting (strategy, advertising, and HR). While most of those we

interviewed were seasoned "rainmakers" in their field, we did speak with a handful of individuals at the beginning and midway points of their careers. We spoke with individuals at some of the largest firms in their industry and also with professionals at midsized, boutique, and solo firms. Finally, we spoke with professionals who bought professional services.

2. A review of the existing literature, both academic and popular, on the subject of business development for consulting and professional services. There are some strong materials out there. Three of our favorites are Ford Harding's *Rain Making*, Arthur Gensler's *Art's Principles*, and Mike Schultz and John Doerr's *Professional Services Marketing*. Our hope is that what we have written here builds on their work and contributes to the ongoing conversation about what works and what doesn't.

Attention Scholars

This book is *not* intended to be an academic publication. It's a book for and by practitioners. The breadth and depth of our research is not statistically weighty enough to be included in a peer-reviewed academic journal, nor are either of us PhD scientists, economists, or psychologists. That said, to the world of academia, we would say, "Jump in. The water's warm." The subject of how those with expertise engage with those they can most help in a highly distributed global world is ripe for further study.

3. Our collective experience working in management consulting and business services for fifty years. We looked to our own personal experiences in our consulting practices to

capture what we had learned and share it. It was encouraging to us that much of what we feel is true was echoed in what we heard from those we interviewed.

Onward

Your expertise deserves to find an audience—the exact right audience where what you know and what you've seen (and you've seen some stuff) will find a home where it can create value, not just for you, but more importantly, for the people whom you most want to serve.

The world needs your expertise. Let's dig in and learn how to build a better bridge to those that could use it.

CHAPTER

Finders, Minders, and Grinders

The Business Development Imperative

When Russell Davis first heard the news, he flew home from Switzerland early. Word had come to him from all directions—the foreign edition of CNN, urgent phone calls from home, and emotional email bursts from friends on campus.

In a convulsion of violence, a mentally disturbed student shot and killed thirty-two students in the Norris and West Ambler Johnston halls at Virginia Tech. It was mid-April of 2007 and Russell was studying abroad, but he was also class president and a dyed-in-the-wool Hokie.

"I felt I needed to go home and be with everyone."

The next few weeks were filled with emotions for Russell and for his fellow students, a complicated stew of anger at the shooter, grief over the lost promise of those who had been slain, and relief and guilt over having not been a target. Russell remembers trying to frame the right words for his address to the graduating class in May.

"I wanted to be careful; it was a commencement, not a funeral," he said. In the end, standing in front of five thousand graduates at Worsham Field, he spoke from the heart, "You only live once. Never waste a moment."

Russell showed leadership in the way he chose to be with those whom he had decided to serve. It wasn't like Mel Gibson on a stallion, rallying of the Scottish tribes in *Braveheart*, but a quieter call to duty, which becomes the standard against which the rest of us measure ourselves.

At Virginia's Darden School of Business, where Russell earned an MBA after Virginia Tech, roughly half of the students apply for jobs at the big consulting firms. Of those, half get interviews, and then half of them get offers. It is the same at all the leading business schools.

Boston Consulting Group (BCG), one of the country's premier strategy consulting firms, has a mission to "go deep to unlock insight and have the courage to act." For that, they need leaders and strong thinkers who have the courage of their convictions. When they first met Russell on the campus of the University of Virginia, they must have known they'd found a real leader, recruiting him to be a summer intern in between years at business school. Later, when he graduated, BCG asked him to sign on, full-time, as a consultant.

Getting hired by one of the big consulting firms is, for many, like winning the lottery. "BCG and the others would come in and make presentations to the students and talk about the cool strategy work they did for clients. I knew I would learn a lot in consulting and that it would open doors. Those of us who got offers were pretty excited. BCG, McKinsey, and Bain have a line out the door to get in. They get the best and brightest."

Consulting

Consulting draws some of the best business school students because consultants are called in to do challenging and essential work. "Since working at BCG," reports Russell, "I've worked on growth strategy, cost reduction, and operations projects in consumer products, transportation, and industrial goods. I've learned a lot in two years. I travel a fair bit, but the firm treats me well and I make good money."

Really good money.

The average starting salary for a post-MBA graduate like Russell at BCG is $147,000 with another $50,000 to $70,000 piled on top in bonuses and 401(k) contributions. This wage is not the exception but the rule at the most prestigious firms like Bain, McKinsey, Oliver Wyman, L.E.K., and A. T. Kearney. It's the same with the Big Four professional services firms, where KPMG, Deloitte, E&Y, and PWC all pay total compensation north of $150,000 for recent MBA graduates, as do the big IT consulting firms like Accenture and IBM.

I'm Not Even in That Universe

If you are a sole proprietor, work for a small CPA firm, or have just hung up your shingle as an attorney, Russell's world may seem distant and vaguely exotic, like GN-z11, the galaxy Hubble just discovered at the far reaches of space. Interesting but not really relevant. You hear about hundreds of thousands of dollars in *pay*, and you think to yourself, "hundreds of thousands of dollars of *revenue* would be good."

We understand. Both of us have been sole proprietors. Tom remembers launching a private equity firm and wondering if the deals would come in. "I'd lie awake at night thinking about the kids and the next mortgage payment and see blood dripping from the ceiling." Doug remembers flying out to New York to make a big client pitch and wondering if he had made some sort of tragic mistake leaving the security of a job at General Electric to launch his fledgling consultancy.

Stick with us. We're digging into the world of high-end consultants for a reason. It turns out their problems are the same as ours, and in their experience, there are clues as to how clients buy.

The Ladder

Russell learned a few things about consulting while working at BCG. "There's a distinct ladder. As a new consultant, there's an expectation that you get up to speed quickly, and that you contribute quickly. If you join BCG right out of undergrad, they call you an associate. If you get promoted from that or join post-MBA, you're a consultant. After consultant, you become a project leader where you manage a team and probably have a couple of consultants and maybe an associate working with you. Two years after being a project leader, you might get promoted to principal and have two project leaders working under you. If you work as a principal for between three and five years, you'd be eligible to stand for election to the partnership. Then as a partner, you might be promoted to senior partner and possibly to the firm's leadership."

While the titles might be different if you are in an architecture or law firm, the idea is the same. First you toil with the rest of the recent grads, and if you are good, you advance one rung on the ladder at a time. And the firm makes it worth your time. Partners at BCG make seven figures with bonuses and profit sharing. If you're a kid from Staunton, Virginia, like Russell, that has your full attention and absolute dedication.

Up or Out

The second lesson Russell learned at BCG was harsher. "It's up or out here. The messaging starts as soon as you get here. 'Look around you,' they say, 'there are not as many partners as there are consultants. Do the math: not everyone can be partner.' Everyone talks about it," he says.

"You know you'll either be promoted or you'll get the boot, though no one ever really gets fired. Instead you hear someone left the firm to take on an 'opportunity in industry.' What you don't hear is that it wasn't 100% their choice. And it happens on every step on the ladder. There is constant pruning."

Everyone who enters into BCG is taught this basic lesson and so begins to ask the natural question, "What do I need to do to succeed here?" It is a Darwinian meritocracy in which only the best survive. Everyone else is "counseled out." It's all very polite, but large consulting firms are built to be unforgiving pyramids in which not everyone can succeed.

The Cravath System

Paul Cravath was born in Ohio in the summer of 1861. A graduate of the Oberlin College and Columbia Law, he would tell fellow New York attorneys that Cravath was derived from the Czech word for "tailor," which itself came from the word for "cut." It would always get a chuckle because his friends knew him to be a fan of managing his law firm by cutting underperforming professionals.

Cravath towered over his colleagues at 6'4". A name partner in the firm now known as Cravath, Swaine & Moore, he served clients like Chemical Bank, Bethlehem Steel, and the Studebaker Corporation and was known as one of the most respected attorneys in the country. He had very clear ideas about how a law firm should be run, ideas which were not commonplace. His approach became known as the "Cravath System."

- Hire the best attorneys from the best law schools. Look to grades as a way of predicting success in the law.
- Pay them well. Up until Cravath, young attorneys apprenticed themselves, trading their time for training. To pay young attorneys was revolutionary.
- Train them extensively by rotating them between assignments. Cravath did not believe in silos. He thought broadly experienced attorneys brought the most value to clients.
- Reward merit. Cravath believed in running his firm as a meritocracy. Young attorneys were promoted for being successful, or if they did not make the cut, they were dismissed.

Today, nearly all consulting and professional services firms are managed this way. Cravath's system has become ubiquitous for three important reasons:

- **Leverage:** Partners can get paid more if they do not just bill out at their hourly rate but also take a slice of what their junior associates bill out for. If you just bill out at your rate, there is a cap on what you can make, but if you act like a value-added reseller of other people's time, there's no limit to what you can make. Your pay is only a function of the size of the assignments you find and the number of people required to do the work. It's the business model.

- **Motivation:** Young associates will work longer hours, grinding away with enthusiasm, if they feel one day their reward might be millions of dollars and a membership at the Greenwich Country Club. Also, they know if they don't, they'll be fired. Call it the carrot and cudgel approach.

- **Quality:** It's hard to hire well. Using top law schools as an initial screen on who is good and who is not saves time.

The Three-Legged Stool

Over beers on the weekend, Russell and his newly minted colleagues would talk about what it takes to get ahead at BCG.

The first leg, and everyone agrees on this point, is you must be good at the work. This goes for every kind of professional service: law or IT consulting as well as the more rarified world of strategy consulting. No one gets from the first to the second rung without doing a good job at delivering the service that is embedded in the promise of their firm. Accenture is the largest IT consultant in the world. If Accenture says it will produce actionable data from multiple sources in and outside of a business, you must be able to do that for clients, or Accenture (and you) will get fired.

The second leg is team leadership. You must be able to rodeo others on a team who are delivering the work. If a Seattle-based CPA firm sends a group of professionals to audit the books at a cannery in Alaska, they'll send a team leader to keep everyone driving in the same direction. She'll also get to pick where everyone has drinks after work.

Both of these skills—doing the work and leading others in the delivery of work—have beginning, intermediate, advanced, and master versions. Fixing the e-commerce site of a $30 million dollar retailer of sporting goods is hard. Our friends at Accenture tell us that fixing HealthCare.gov was harder. The first job was a blue square groomer, the second a black diamond pitch off the backside.

The third leg of the stool is the ability to generate new business. It's one thing to be able to do the work well and to lead successful engagement, but someone in the firm has to be the one who spoke with the client in the first place, inking the deal that got the work.

Art Gensler, author of *Art's Principles* and founder of Gensler—the premier design and architecture firm that designed the Apple Store—says, "Business rarely falls into your lap. You must go out, explore, and find clients."

The Commercial Imperative

They say in consulting and professional services that there are "finders, minders, and grinders." Grinders do the work. Minders supervise the grinders. Finders bring in the work on which everyone else delivers.

Russell is clear on this rainmaker imperative. "By the time you are a partner, you need to have a commercial focus. You need to come across as credible and be able to sell a multimillion-dollar transformation to a company."

But to know what to do is not to know how to do it. "If I had one question for a senior partner at the firm," says Russell, "it would be 'How did they find their best clients?' Most of the work at a big firm like BCG comes from repeat business and from referrals, but I would be interested in knowing what the partner did, especially in the early years, to find those big clients that hire us over and over."

We find this question interesting as well.

The Rest of Us

This question of how to find new work is not limited to the big firms. It's common to all consultants or professional service providers. While website designers or freelance cybersecurity specialists might not be working in the Cravath salt mines at a 10,000-person professional services firm, they experience their own version of "up or out." They either bring in new work or they fail.

"If I don't sell, I am out of business," says Megan Armstrong, the owner of a three-person marketing communications company. "Without clients, there's no work."

It's really just a variation on the same theme: to be successful in consulting and professional services, you have to be a grinder, a minder, and a finder. It is the platform on which all of us stand. If you're weak at any one of these three disciplines, the stool will not support your weight. If you're at a big firm, it means you'll wash out and not make partner. If you're a sole proprietor, your enterprise will fail.

Okay, I Need to Sell; How Do I Do That?

Saying that those in consulting and professional services need to think about where their next meal is coming from is not a controversial statement. How to do that, as we will see, is controversial. Some see expert services as just another product that can be sold like a pen or a load of lumber. Others, and we are in this camp, see consulting and professional services as very different, requiring a unique approach.

Russell knows that he has to learn how to go out and find business if he is going to make it in this world of consulting. He also knows it's going to be hard. It's a skill he didn't learn in business school. So we took his question to the best in this business. We interviewed some of the most accomplished pros and learned why selling consulting and professional services is a challenge. In the next chapter, we will work to better understand how consulting and professional service practitioners engage with would-be clients is different from the way other goods are sold. The goal is not to sell what we do but to be invited by clients into their projects as trusted partners.

Obstacles

3

Beyond Pixels

Selling a Service Is Different from Selling Things (and Harder, too)

Selling high-end expert services is different from selling ice cream or iPads.

Economists call consulting and professional services "credence goods." Asher Wolinsky, a microeconomics professor at Northwestern University, puts it this way:

The term credence good refers to goods and services whose sellers are also experts who determine the customers' needs. This feature is shared by medical and legal services and a wide variety of business services. In such markets, even when the success of performing the service is observable, customers often cannot determine the extent of the service that was needed and how much was actually performed.

We all know the feeling. You drop off your laptop at the repair shop in the mall because you woke up on Monday morning to the blue screen of death. There is a nice guy there whose job it is to wrangle customers. He tells you he will call you later once they look under the hood. You suspect he was hired because he is a smooth talker and not because he really knows anything about computers. It feels like his job is to keep you away from the tech guys.

He calls you mid-morning.

"We took a look at your laptop. Your memory board is most likely fried. We're going to run a diagnostic test and that will help us better understand what is going on, but I wanted to warn you that it might require a new memory board."

You search for the right way to respond. "It's just over a year old." You are whispering into your cell because you are on site at a client. "Why did this happen?"

"It is actually fairly common with this computer. The company claims there are no manufacturing defects, but we see the same problem in here all the time. It was a bad batch of chips from a startup manufacturer in Taiwan. Depending on what we find, you might get away with just adding a memory board. Or it could require a new motherboard, which is not going to be cheap. Next time you may want to consider the extended warranty."

"Okay," you say weakly. "Give me a call when you are done with the diagnostic."

"Will do."

You are in the hands of an expert and totally at their mercy.

It's the same thing at the doctor. "Let me consult with some of my colleagues and then we can talk about therapy options. . . ."

It is a queasy, helpless feeling. They are the experts, and they are both defining the problem and making a recommendation. Dr. Wolinsky calls this "information asymmetry." One side knows everything, and the other side knows what they Googled on WebMD.

This asymmetry is one of the reasons selling legal services is a lot like selling cybersecurity expertise, even though the lawyer's capabilities are very different from those of the security consultant. All expert service providers sell services under circumstances in which the client has to *trust* them implicitly.

Think about when you speak with an attorney about using a boilerplate nondisclosure form you got off the Internet. Businesses have been swapping NDAs for decades, you say. Surely they're all the same. Inevitably, though, your attorney uses their expertise to point out that the generic form you found on www.howhardcanlawbeafterall.com doesn't actually cover your specific business. "Because your intellectual property resides in Ireland, we will need to include a section to make sure you are protected there. Also, we will need to change the arbitration clause."

Chagrined, you say something like, "Well, why don't you look it over and do what needs to be done." Two days later you get a red-lined version and a bill for 3.4 billable hours. It's in that moment that you understand *exactly* what Dr. Wolinsky means when he writes, "Customers often cannot determine the extent of the service that was needed and how much was actually performed."

The word, "credence" comes from the Latin word *credere*, a verb that means *to believe* or *to trust*. It is a root that has given rise to words like creditor (someone who trusts you) and credibility (a quality assigned to someone worthy of trust). When you buy credence goods, you have to trust the expert in whom you put your care.

Selling Consulting and Professional Services Is Hard Because Our Clients Have to Trust Us Before They Buy from Us

Clients must believe the expert will diagnose their problem correctly.

Clients must believe the expert will prescribe an effective solution.

Clients must believe the expert can and will do the work in a way that will achieve the outcome they want.

Clients have to believe the expert will fairly price the service based on work actually done.

The Three R's

Credence goods are sold on trust. It is the electricity that powers engagement between experts and those they most want to serve. Trust is transmitted from one person to another in three ways:

- **Relationships**—I go to church with an attorney and know her to be a good person.
- **Referral**—I have a friend whom I trust, and he recommends the web developer over in the tech park. He says I should ask for Ann.
- **Reputation**—I read in the *Village Wrap* that Criterion Solutions was voted #1 in HR consulting for the second year in a row.

These are the ways clients buy. Clients hire people they know, respect, and trust or who come recommended by a close friend or colleague.

How Services Are Different

Now think about how products are sold.

You're sick of your iPhone. The microphone keeps going on the fritz and apps randomly slip off of the screen. To be fair, you did drop it on the pavement in Dallas two weeks ago. You get online and search for "best phones," and after scrolling past the sponsored ads, you see reviews by CNET and *PC Magazine* where phones are ranked by various attributes—speed, weight, reliability, cost, picture quality, and battery life. You look at that list and give each attribute your own weight. "I care about battery life a lot, but I don't care about camera quality or price."

You scan through the comparative tables and allow yourself to be colored by the reviewers' florid prose either advocating for the phone or against it. Then you make a choice.

There would be information asymmetry between you and the phone manufacturer—you don't know anything really about how phones work—but two forces intervene:

- CNET and *PC Magazine* volunteer to act as impartial information intermediaries.
- The attributes can be objectively quantified. Cost is known. Battery life can be tested.

The result is that, at least partially, you're able to buy a phone rationally and not overly rely on relationships, referrals, or reputation to drive your decision. We say "overly" because, of course, this distinction is not binary. Lots of us call up friends and ask, "What phone should I buy?" or buy based on a brand relationship.

There is always a push in consulting and professional services to make credence goods more like regular goods. The market intelligence firm Gartner has made a good business of ranking IT professional services firms according to completeness of vision and ability to execute in an effort to create a CNET analog for IT service buyers.

"Completeness of vision" and "ability to execute" are more difficult to quantify than speed or camera quality and are somewhat subjective criteria. You can do a bench test on a phone and measure processor speed and pixels per square inch. Still, using a proprietary algorithm, Gartner divides tech service firms into Leaders, Challengers, Visionaries, and Niche Players in an attempt to provide guidance to buyers.

But this effort to make buying more rational does not take away the wider truth that clients engage with those they trust when handing over something important to an expert who will both diagnose the problem and make a recommendation on what to do—whether that is a doctor or web designer, compensation specialist, or plant security consultant.

David Maister, the former Harvard Business School professor, who for two decades was widely acknowledged as the world's leading authority on the management of professional services firms, shares this point of view:

> The need for trust in dealings with clients should be obvious. Consider your own purchases of professional services. Whether you are hiring someone to look after your legal affairs, your taxes, your child or your Porsche, the act of retaining a professional requires you to put your affairs in someone else's hands. You are forced into an act of faith, and you can only hope that they will deal with you appropriately.

You can research their background, check their technical skills and attempt to examine their past performance. In spite of all this, when it comes down to making the final decision on whom to hire you must ultimately decide to trust someone with your baby—which is never a comfortable thing to have to do.

David's perspective resonates with us. If your parents are in need of a will and you volunteer to help them find an attorney, it is most likely you won't Google, "best attorney in Miami." Likewise, you're unlikely to ring up the number of an attorney whose phone number you saw on a billboard or the side of truck.

The way you'd find your folks a good attorney is by recommending someone with whom you worked, or you would call a friend who is an attorney and ask for their recommendation. Or use a combination of both: "I used this great attorney at work for our mergers work. I asked her who she would recommend."

Note to Millennials

If you were born from the early 1980s to early 2000s, you are among a demographic group sociologists refer to as Gen Y or Millennials. Marc Prensky, an American writer and speaker on education, calls this generation *digital natives*, arguing that millennials were the first generation to live entirely within the digital era, giving them a comfort with all things digital: cell phones, computers, the Internet, and digital audio/video.

We, Tom and Doug, are both in our early 50s. While comfortable with most things digital, we are not digital natives. We're reasonably fluent users of our smart phones, but when we have questions about our phones (frequently), or an app, or social media, we turn to our digitally native kids, students, or coworkers.

We say this because this book is written to describe how client buying decisions are made today, not how they will be made in 2025 or 2035. Today's corporate decision makers are by and large *not* digital natives. Like us, most of today's corporate leaders were born before the digital era began. Therefore, independent of how comfortable today's leaders are with phones and apps, our generation does not rely on their phones or laptops for making decisions in the same way that a millennial might.

We recently spoke with Erin, who was helping us with edits on this book. She's in her mid-thirties and teaches English at a local university. We were explaining to her that we believe clients hire people whom they *know, respect, and trust*—or who come highly recommended by a close friend or colleague.

Erin had an entirely different take. She shared with us that she typically uses Yelp or other crowd-sourced review data when making decisions about a doctor or attorney. She quipped, "My friends wouldn't know which attorney to use if I asked them. I would rather trust Yelp." That got us into a lively conversation. We took the view that Yelp might be useful in choosing a restaurant, but when a decision is big and consequential, that is a different matter. Still, life is changing. One day, *How Clients Buy* may be quite different from what it is today.

Product and credence goods are sold very differently. Clients do not buy credence goods based on features or attributes; they buy consulting and professional services based on *intangible* criteria.

Product Sales	Credence Goods
Tangible	Intangible
Specifications	Reputation
Attributes	Credibility
Features	Respect
Warranty	Thought Leadership
Promotions	Relationship
Brick and Mortar/Internet	Trust

Supply and Demand

We all took microeconomics in college. We were taught that price has two drivers—supply and demand. If there is limited supply, say of Taylor Swift tickets at the CenturyLink Field, then as demand goes up, so does price. That's why you can find Taylor Swift tickets on StubHub for upwards of $500. Likewise, if there is a limited amount of demand, say for Fortune 500 companies interested in conducting a strategic review (there are only 500 of them), you would expect prices to go down as the number of strategy consultants goes up.

But that's not the case. In consulting and professional services, the price rarely correlates with either supply or demand. It's because we sell credence goods. Economists tell us that in credence good transactions, it is hard for clients to value quality. The expert, after all, knows more than we do, both about our problems and how to solve them. For this reason, reputation stands in as a proxy for quality.

Fish & Richardson, for example, has a reputation for being one of the very best intellectual property law firms. Because of this, they can charge huge sums per hour despite the fact that intellectual property law is taught at every law school and there are 1.2 million lawyers in the United States.

The fact that the laws of supply and demand do not hold in the world of consulting and professional services suggests that the way we sell those services is different from the way we sell shoes.

Systemic Hurdles

We've just described why selling consulting and professional services is different from selling a product—and harder, too. But it is worse than you think. In addition to the very nature of the consulting and professional service sale being different from selling products, there are four systemic obstacles that stand in the way of us getting good at selling services.

Let us try to understand these obstacles because the seeds of a new way of thinking about selling consulting and professional services must grow in this rocky soil. Understanding each of these obstacles is necessary so we know what we are up against before putting till to ground and learn how to better cultivate the kind of new clients that will cause our practices to grow and thrive.

4

Obstacle #1: What They Didn't Teach You in B-School

If I Am Supposed to Be the Expert, Why Do I Feel So Stupid about Sales?

George Wythe was one of the most respected attorneys in colonial Virginia. The Reverend Lee Massey called him "the only honest lawyer I ever knew." That reputation caused Wythe to be in great demand. The anteroom in his Williamsburg office was filled with farm owners contesting boundaries, gentlemen hoping to draft bills of sale, and sea captains settling debts. In 1762, he decided he needed help. He'd learned the law working for his uncle, Stephen Dewey, in Prince George's County, and thought it made sense for him to see if there was a young man at the College of William and Mary he might take on in a similar role. The deal would be that he would teach the lad the law, and in exchange the apprentice would help with drafting. He met his friend Dr. William Small, a Scotsman who taught at the college. Over several rounds of rattle-skulls, a popular brandy and porter cocktail, at the Raleigh Tavern, he asked his friend for a recommendation. Putting his drink down, Small didn't hesitate. "Young Tom Jefferson from Shadwell is your boy. His mother is a Randolph, and he's quite intelligent."

This model of standing next to the person you want to become was familiar to both Wythe and Jefferson. It was the way blacksmiths, candle makers, apothecaries, coopers, tinkers, limners, wheelwrights, wainwrights, bakers, and silversmiths were trained. Want to build houses? Work for a housemaker. Want to be a lawyer? Work for a lawyer.

For much of American history, apprenticeship was the main model for training attorneys, accountants, architects, doctors, and engineers. You clerked for an accomplished professional, learned by observing what they did, and exchanged your labor for their knowledge and oversight. After becoming a master and able to serve clients on your own, you would set up shop in a new location so as not to compete.

An important part of the apprenticeship education was an understanding of how to attract new clients. We, of course, have no record of Wythe's advice to Thomas Jefferson on this score, but judging by their action and legacy, we imagine he said something like, "Do good work, be honest in all your relations, be civically active, write for publication, and never turn down a chance to speak in public."

Universities

The way of educating young professionals through apprenticeship changed once universities started offering degree programs to students in fields like law, accounting, and engineering. Business education soon followed with universities starting to award Masters of Business Administration. In a short time, professional certifying groups like the legal and accounting associations started to communicate that the preferred way to be trained in those professions was to go to school.

Somewhere in that transition from apprenticeship to university-led training, the focus on how to engage with clients was lost. Today, we are left with a situation where earning credentials in your field means that you know how to *deliver* work but don't necessarily know how to *sell* that work.

That bears repeating:

Selling insights, design, expertise, and advice is NOT something you were taught in the classroom.

Doug knows. He's a professor of business. "We teach students accounting, computer science, engineering but not how to sell those services. Sales is the pariah of the academic world."

That is because sales, as a discipline, is thought to be beneath the academy.

While business schools have continued to offer some type of sales management instruction—usually within a larger marketing course—they do not offer courses in salesmanship skills. The topic remains, just as it was in the 1910s, more suitable for popular how-to books and memoirs of successful salespeople than for academic classes.

—Walter Friedman, *Birth of a Salesman: The Transformation of Selling in America*

Here's the first-year MBA curriculum at Wharton, grouped into six categories of classes:

- Leadership: Foundations of Teamwork and Leadership
- Marketing: Marketing Management
- Microeconomics: Microeconomic Foundation
- Economics: Advanced Topics in Managerial Economics
- Statistics: Regression Analysis for Managers
- Management Communication: Speaking and Writing

Nothing on selling or business development. Odd, you think; your dad's voice rings in your head, "Nothing ever happens unless somebody sells something." To be fair, he was in insurance, but still, you'd think there'd be a course on how to sell at a business school. Doesn't every company have a sales division? Aren't one out of every twenty Americans employed in some kind of sales job?

Other professional schools like architecture, law, or accounting also ignore sales. Flip through the Stanford Law School catalog, and you will see courses in mergers and acquisitions and in administrative, environmental, criminal, and intellectual property law, but you won't find a sales course.

What gives? Don't professionals run businesses, and don't businesses need customers?

The dirty little secret of professional finishing schools is that they equip you to do the work, but they give you little guidance on how to find customers.

This situation is okay if you are a junior person at a large consulting or professional services firm. The senior people will feed you work and keep you busy toiling in the basement without rest, but . . .

- if you want to be a senior person, you will need to learn about how to effectively find new business.

- if you spin out and start your own firm, you will need to learn about how to effectively find new business.
- if at any point in your future, you want to stop being at the bottom of the totem pole, grinding away at work passed down from on high, you will need to learn how to effectively find new business.

It's crazy if you think about it—that we would invest hundreds of thousands of dollars into making sure we have the skills to help clients when they walk in the door but not a cent on making sure the hinges on the door are well oiled.

Historically, training of professionals to win new clients has been haphazard. Law, accounting, engineering, medical, and architectural schools teach nothing about selling. This is also true of most business schools, surprisingly so, given that a sale is what defines the existence of a business. Many firms offer in-house education on technical issues, and almost all provide such training on the job, but marketing and sales training is spotty. Most of us must learn by trial and error.

—Ford Harding, *Rain Making*

Why Business Schools Do Not Teach How to Sell Professional Services

If you want to become a professor of philosophy, there is a thousand-year history of being trained and credentialed by a university as a PhD. Not so with consultants and professional services providers. Their credentialing is a very recent phenomenon. It was only in 1887 that thirty-one accountants decided to band together to create the American Association of Public Accountants to set standards for their profession and to begin to test would-be accountants on their proficiency.

Universities, too, came into the act relatively recently, and when they did, their newly created business schools struggled for academic legitimacy.

> We have no record of a business school in the New World before the landing of the Pilgrim Fathers. The earliest we know of was founded in Plymouth in 1635, probably a transplant from a thriving British industry. Mr. Morton, its proprietor, advertised reading, writing, and the casting of accounts. For two centuries and a half after that, business schools remained purely vocational, concentrating on 'penmanship, bookkeeping, rapid methods of making computations, and grammatical construction and composition of mercantile correspondence.'
>
> —Richard Rosett, former Dean, Graduate
> School of Business at the University of Chicago

Then at the turn of the last century, a new class of business school emerged, offering advanced courses and broadening their scope away from the techniques of business to include best practices in business. Rosett says:

> Chicago's dean in 1928, Leon Carroll Marshall, described a new sort of business professor who would "devote [himself] to the study and presentation of the fundamental processes, conditions, and forces of 'business with quite incidental attention to minor techniques.'" Marshall advised that, "business education calls for mature contacts with several existing scientific disciplines . . . the economics of today should place emphasis upon quantitative analysis and upon such . . . borderlands as between economics and law, or between economics and psychology."

This push away from the practical and toward the theoretical caught fire, and soon business schools were offering not only

MBAs but PhDs in business. Like other social sciences, including sociology, anthropology, and psychology, the study of business suffered from an inferiority complex as newcomers in the academic ranks. Business departments made up for it by emulating the hard sciences like mathematics and physics, teaching economics, finance, the management of resources—anything that could be quantified—while eschewing soft skills like people management or sales, which might be better learned standing at the side of an experienced practitioner.

Sales—the art of finding and engaging with a would-be client—became a relic like computation and penmanship that was best left to vocational "Schools of Commerce."

And so few of us were trained in how to sell consulting or professional services. This is ironic. As a nation, we pride ourselves on being at the leading edge of business. We love showcasing technology companies at our business schools. And yet companies like Oracle, SAP, and Microsoft were built on effective salesforces in addition to great technology. Companies like Google and Facebook, while not as salesforce-intensive, are in the business of helping other businesses sell.

The result of this is that when we think about the need to increase our business by doing more business development, our stomach tightens. It is not something we were taught.

"I wish the quality of my work would be enough to grow my practice."

"I hate sales. It's beneath me."

"I'm not a marketing person."

"Whenever I try and wade into business development, I feel like I don't know what I'm doing."

If you are having those thoughts, stop beating yourself up. You are confusing your lack of confidence with your lack of training. Tom goes golfing with his company every July. It used to make him tense because he is not a golfer. Four or five times later, though, he was having fun (they're scrambles). This is the nature of humans when they move out of their comfort zone and then expand that zone as they acquire new skills.

Relax. You were taught how to help clients with your expertise, but no one ever said, "Here's how you attract new clients." You wouldn't expect employees to do a good job on a new task for which they hadn't been trained. Don't judge yourself by a different standard.

5

Obstacle #2: But I Don't Want to Sell

Moving Past Willy Loman

A fire hydrant of a man, Chuck Alpine stood square, brimming with the kind of red-faced passion you'd expect from a former TV star and bodybuilder-cum-fitness club entrepreneur.

> I could sell a ketchup popsicle to a lady wearing white gloves in the middle of July. You can be goddamn sure I can sell gym memberships.

The room grew quiet.

Chuck sat at the head of a heavy boardroom table in a small windowless room. Behind him, a two-foot, all-gold screaming eagle rested on a counter. To his right hung a poster, featuring an elephant on its feet reaching for tree leaves; underneath was the phrase: "Goals: The difference between try and triumph is a little umph."

Chuck owns a chain of fitness clubs spread across the industrial Midwest. He was born in Texas, so it's not surprising that his clubs are big, mostly retrofits of old supermarkets, full of dozens of treadmills, TRX-friendly superstructures, even wind tunnels for cooling off.

He's explaining his successful twenty-seven-club chain to investors, a pair of thirty-somethings scribbling notes.

"I grew up in the fitness business. Started in Texas out of high school. Then moved to southern California. This is a sales business. Don't let anyone tell you differently. MBAs'll tell you clubs are about retention, that we lose half our customers a year, but that's bull crap. The only way this business works is if you get out on the floor and sell."

A slim man wearing chinos and a dark blue blazer lifts his head up from a yellow pad. "Tell us more about your customer acquisition strategy. How are you able to teach associates how to sell so effectively?"

Chuck squints at the man, a vein popping up under his leathery skin.

"You run contests. We always have a summer contest where the clubs compete against each other for a big trip. We make it a big deal. I bring the best team up on a stage and if they win, we give them each a Stetson and talk about how much a stud they are. But it's about human psychology, too. If someone walks in the door and I'm going to sell them, I always show them around the club. I want to talk about our pool and show them how clean the locker rooms are, but I also want to soften them up before I sit them down in the sales pit."

Chuck warms to his story, a smile starting to crawl across his face. He leans back, fingers laced behind his head. His hair is shiny, like he might use product.

"I ask them what their goals are. Most important part of the pitch. Do they want to lose weight? Are they looking to spice up their social life? Do they have a reunion coming up? There's always something. I use that to sell. I store it in my brain for later if they start to object. They might say, for example, 'That's too much for my budget.'

"I say, 'I understand,' and then I get all sad looking and say, 'I thought you were serious about losing weight because you wanted to get back out there. You serious about getting back out there?' I tie it back to what they said their motivation was. It's not my motivation, it's their motivation and once they give that up to me, I can just beat them around the ears with it. I've never had it not work," he says, his black eyes pushing out to make the point. "I always tell our guys if you can't sell $2,000 worth of personal training to a forty-five-year-old lawyer who has a paunch, just got divorced and is looking to meet women, you aren't really trying."

You've met Chuck before—maybe not at the fitness club but at the auto dealership or condo sales office. There are Chucks all around us, and they are our second obstacle because *we don't want to be Chuck*.

Do you agree? What do you think of the woman at the dealership who tries to upsell you to the cold-weather package and undercarriage protection? The guy at the mall jewelry store that peers over the glass counter and says, "We find a good rule of thumb is that you should spend about three months' salary on an engagement ring. Not sure what you make, but I wanted to show you this $15,000 princess cut."

Be honest because it is helpful to put a name on what you do not want to be.

If you are like us, you think of salespeople as the bottom-feeders of commerce. In a charitable moment, we might think they are a necessary evil at car dealerships and mall jewelry stores, but we'd be quick to say that there is no room for a salesperson in consulting or professional services. That is because we think our world is above salespeople. We "engage" with would-be clients. We don't sell. Selling is manipulative.

We're not alone in this view. Every year the Gallup Poll conducts a survey asking which professions are thought to be honest and ethical. Estimable professions include nurses, pharmacists, doctors, engineers, fire fighters, and clergy. At the other end of the spectrum skulk members of Congress, HMO managers, and—you knew this was coming—salespeople. The lowest seven professions included car salespeople, insurance salespeople, advertising executives, and stockbrokers.

That is because most of us believe that sales is the art of:

Causing someone to take an action they wouldn't take if left to their own devices.

It's no wonder we think of salespeople as odious and can't imagine joining their ranks.

Why We Can Never Imagine Being Salespeople

Most people dislike the idea of "selling" because selling sits at the intersection of the following three ideas.

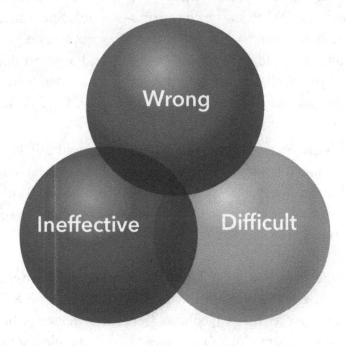

Why We Dislike Selling

Most of us think sales is:

- **Wrong**: Consulting and professional service providers feel like selling is inconsistent with their commitment to professional ethics. If selling means causing others to do what they might not do if left to their own devices, and professionalism is doing what is best for the client at all times, then there is an inherent conflict between selling and being a professional.

- **Ineffective**: Nearly all the consulting and professional services pros we interviewed said they felt that traditional sales techniques wouldn't work on their clients. Unlike the old door-to-door vacuum cleaner sales pitch perfected in the 1950s, no one dumps dirt on the carpet of a potential client's office to demonstrate the effectiveness of their vacuum cleaner/digital transformation. We spoke with Jane Pierce, who left ADM to start a consulting practice. She remembers what it was like to get calls from salespeople as a potential client. "I wouldn't even take a call. I had a guard dog that blocked out all of those calls. I figured if I needed something, I'd go out and look for it. In the meantime, I didn't have the time."

- **Difficult:** Sales is hard work. Salespeople cold call, knock on the doors of people they don't know, bear near-constant rejection. Sales is out of our comfort zone. We know accounting, the law, or IT security, but not how to sell that knowledge.

Who wants to live at what John Venn called the center of his "Eulerian Circles"—that place where what is wrong, ineffective, and hard intersect? Brian Jacobsen, general manager of business operations at Slalom Consulting, says "I think people are hesitant to sell. There is something caught up in that word, 'selling.'"

To put a cherry on all this, most of us harbor feelings that sales is *déclassé* and beneath us.

> I don't want to be called a salesperson. That feels more like the woman at Lord & Taylor in a white blouse and black skirt helping you buy a pocketbook.
> —Audrey Cramer, Vice Chairman,
> Cushman and Wakefield

We are told that people who have higher degrees manage salespeople. They are never salespeople themselves. Most professionals resolve the cognitive dissonance between the need to grow their business and their feelings that sales is inappropriate to consulting and professional services practices by taking a hard line against sales.

Walt Shill, formerly of McKinsey and Accenture, shared this story:

> A long time ago at McKinsey, before paved roads and electricity, we didn't use the word 'sell.' We didn't even use the word sales. We recorded professional fees and so there was this view that clients have problems and we need to discover, understand, and tackle them. And the way you do that is you build relationships and you demonstrate the capability to solve problems. And then once people realize you help them solve problems, then they will come back.

The Birth of Management Consulting

A kid from Cleveland, Marvin Bower put himself through Brown by working for a law firm that specialized in debt collection in the wholesale hardware business. He quickly realized that showing up at a warehouse and talking to the owner was more effective than sending dunning notices on ornate legal stationery. He'd sit down with the executives and reason with them, explaining the costs of going to court and the virtues of working through the problem with a payment plan. Later, on the advice of his father, Marvin enrolled in Harvard Law School. Getting into Harvard Law wasn't hard then, but as he liked to say, staying in was. "They flunked people all the time."

After graduation, he had his heart set on joining Jones, Day, Reavis and Pogue, the most prestigious law firm in Cleveland, but didn't have the grades. Instead, he enrolled in Harvard Business School, thinking it would make him unique to have both a law and business degree. It did, and upon graduation, he joined Jones Day as a young associate. By this time, companies were starting to get sucked under by the Depression. With his experience in debt collection and his education in law and business, he was soon given the assignment of chairing bankruptcy committees and charged with reorganizing companies like TRW, Studebaker, and Midland Steel.

What he found shocked him. Ten out of the eleven companies he worked with shouldn't have failed. And they wouldn't have if only the CEO had access to the right information. Front-line employees, who saw the truth of their business, were blocked by fear and hierarchy from telling truth to power. The culprit was cultural, not economic.

Marvin's career was going well when, as so often happens with entrepreneurs, bad news forced him in a different direction. Jones Day announced they would be cutting salaries by twenty-five percent. Marvin and his wife sat in an ice cream parlor because it was all they could afford, and decided to move to Chicago, where Marvin joined a small managerial accounting and business analysis firm called McKinsey & Co. Six years later, James McKinsey died unexpectedly and Marvin Bower, along with a partner named A. Tom Kearney, decided to buy the business and focus on helping companies better manage themselves with information and advice.

Marvin's vision was clear: create a professional firm that served clients with the same level of high integrity as law and accounting firms. To him, there was a clear gap in the market. Law firms advised on legal matters, investment bankers on capital, but who was there to advise on how to best manage a company? McKinsey & Co. (and later A.T. Kearney) stepped into the void and the profession now known as management consulting was born.

Marvin took over the helm of McKinsey in 1932 when it had eighteen employees. When he stepped down as managing director in 1967, McKinsey had five hundred employees. Today, that number has swelled to more than 20 thousand.

This type of management consulting was clearly needed, and by any measure, McKinsey & Co. is a very successful company. What's interesting is that even though McKinsey has grown steadily over the years, the company has always taken a dim view of sales. Marvin explained in a 1951 training program, "It is our policy not to solicit clients or advertise our services, not because it is unethical, but because to do so is inconsistent with the professional approach. We can't advertise our services and solicit clients without making implied promises of what we can do for clients. Since we do not, at the outset, know what we can accomplish, such promises do not meet high professional standards." This philosophy permeates the company, and it gives us an important insight into how we must adjust our mindset to help us think about selling professional services as not really selling at all. For Marvin and for McKinsey, the delivery of quality work was the *alpha* and *omega* of business development. Do good work, and your reputation will grow your business.

We Are the Product

We believe the historical aversion to the term selling has a lot to do with the fact that in professional services, we are the product. Unlike those who sell sophisticated software systems to the Fortune 500 or advanced imaging systems to large hospitals, we are selling ourselves. It seems boastful or distasteful to promote ourselves. We've been taught since kindergarten not to be a braggart.

There's a strong, long-held view among the professional services that selling ourselves is unseemly. Promoting ourselves is too crass. Too commercial. Too hucksterish. Many, if not most, of us in professional services have felt this way at some point.

We believe there is a strong need for a better understanding of how to promote ourselves in a way that is effective *and* professional.

Hawkers and Walkers

In his delightful history of sales in the United States, *Birth of Salesman: The Transformation of Selling in America*, Walter Friedman describes how the role of salesperson has evolved over the course of American history.

Peddlers: First there were the young men, eager to leave the farm, who bought inventory, put it in a pack or on the back of horse, and walked from hamlet to hamlet, bartering combs, scissors, pots, and pans for whatever they thought they could sell on "down the line." These early itinerants were an essential distribution network servicing the new American hinterlands with hard goods. Sometimes, though, these eager young men were a little too smooth in their presentation or too forceful as they negotiated their half of the bargain. Friedman shows us that from the first days of the republic, there's been a tension between whether salespeople provided a service or were creatures of self-interest.

Drummers: The industrial revolution brought the rise of corporate traveling salespeople who moved from town to town on behalf of an industrial wholesaler, focusing most of their attention on small business owners who would then retail the goods to consumers. They were said to beat their drum on behalf of their employers, who asked them to live on the road and "drum up" business for the mother company. Drummers were known for their hard drinking, endless supply of jokes, and glad-handing in pursuit of the kind of relationship that they felt fed the long-term recurring sale.

Professional Salespeople: Branded goods like Ivory soap and Heinz 57 began to hire salespeople in the mid-nineteenth century. Because these traveling salespeople needed to be appropriate ambassadors for the brand, these "grips" stepped up their game and began to dress better and cut back on the public house antics. This army was supervised by newly created sales managers who gave us the language we know today: territories, quotas, leads, prequalification, and closing. This professionalization, though, had a dark side as sales professionals lost touch with the value they were bringing to customers and focused on gimmicks that they felt drove certain behaviors. Writes Friedman,

> [So called] cash-register agents in the 1880s learned that people were more likely to buy out of fear of a loss than a promise of gain. [Salesmen] found their most effective sales argument for the cash register to be the "thief catcher campaign." . . . Book canvassers found more success when they revealed only a portion of a book to a farmer, rather than the whole text, thereby heightening the prospect's curiosity. Further, people were more often persuaded to make a purchase if they believed that their neighbors or some prominent people in town, had already bought the product being sold. They did not want to appear unable to keep up with the "Joneses." . . . [Salesmen] knew that prospects were less likely to interrupt a sales spiel if it was accompanied by some simple, seemingly natural, gesture, like digging inside a bag for a free sample or taking off rubber overshoes in anticipation of being let inside out of the rain—as Fuller Brush salesmen did in the 1920s and 1930s.

Friedman calls the development of a salesperson a "uniquely American story," arguing that the combination of industrialization, U.S. geographic scale, and the emergence of credit facilities fueled the trajectory of sales from the amateur and unorganized to the highly coordinated and enabled salesforces of today.

6

Obstacle #3: Things Aren't What They Once Were

It Is Harder Than Ever to Sell Expert Services

John Bates and Van O'Steen graduated from the University of Arizona in 1972, eager and ambitious. Within two years the young men would be known to every lawyer in the country and the subject of hushed conversations in courthouse lobbies and over partner dinners. As they walked across the stage on the day of their graduation, however, they had no idea they were about to rock the world of consulting and professional services.

John and Van couldn't wait to get out of law school and effect social change in a world they saw badly in need of legal help. John had been voted outstanding student and gave the commencement address to his class of 1972. Van had graduated *cum laude* and was an editor on the law journal. Yet instead of cashing in on their honors and going to work for any number of prestigious law firms in Phoenix, they decided to join the Maricopa County Legal Aid Society, where they worked with poor clients. "[We saw] a huge number of people were being turned away [from mainstream law firms] because of lack of financial resources," said John. It upset them both. It wasn't fair that legal expertise was only available to the rich.

They decided to act on their convictions and start their own independent legal clinic dedicated to serving the poor. John and Van wanted to make sure that people could access legal services at an affordable price. Their clinic would offer cut-rate prices on standard legal fare like no-fault divorces, changes in names, personal bankruptcy, and adoption, with the goal of extending high-quality legal assistance to more people, especially those who could least afford it. They were passionate about their work. "We wanted to change the existing system," remembers John.

The newly created firm of Bates and O'Steen quickly realized that in addition to challenging what they saw as the injustice inherent in how legal services were provided, they were also fundamentally changing the dominant business model on which law firms were built. Whereas most firms overcharged for routine work to maintain consistent margins across the practice, John and Van envisioned a low-margin, high-volume practice focused on commonplace tasks. But the door didn't swing like they thought it would. "After two years, we concluded that the clinic would not succeed if we did not advertise," John said. "Because our fees were so low, we needed a greater volume of clients than could be obtained simply by hanging out our shingle and waiting."

On February 22, 1976, they took out an ad in *The Arizona Republic*:

> ### Do you need a lawyer?
> ### Legal services at very reasonable fees
>
> - Divorce or legal separation—uncontested (both spouses sign papers) $175.00 plus $20.00 court filing fee
> - Preparation of all court papers and instructions on how to do your own simple uncontested divorce $100.00
> - Adoption—uncontested severance proceeding $225.00 plus approximately $10.00 publication cost
> - Bankruptcy—non-business, no contested proceedings
>   - Individual $250.00 plus $55.00 court filing fee
>   - Wife and Husband $300.00 plus $110.00 court filing fee
> - Change of Name $95.00 plus $20.00 court filing fee
>
> Information regarding other types of cases furnished upon request. Legal Clinic of Bates & O'Steen

The industry reaction was harsh and immediate, a scorching eruption of censure. The idea of advertising, much less listing prices, was unheard of in the legal community. The Arizona State Bar Association sent the two young men a letter informing them that the bar prohibited practicing attorneys from advertising their services and summoning them to a disciplinary hearing.

Bates and O'Steen argued that by banning advertising, the Arizona bar association was violating the First Amendment and the Sherman Antitrust Act. The bar association knew that this was a high-consequence hearing. At the time, no professional services firms advertised or actively solicited business. It was not considered ethical for professionals whose duty was to protect and advance their clients' interests to take action that might call that loyalty in question by doing something so plainly in their own interests as advertising. Similar strictures were in place for CPAs and other professionals.

Change was in the air, though. Already, the courts had decided that pharmacists—who also have a duty to serve—could reasonably advertise drug specials and some saw that as a break in the dam. Legal experts from around the country were watching the *Bates v. State Bar of Arizona* case to see if the courts would decide if advertising was a kind of commercial free speech that deserved protection.

Drive down the freeway of any large U.S. city, and you know how John and Van fared in court. Peering down from billboards are personal injury attorneys exhorting us to contact them "For a Confidential Case Review." Says one off the Long Island Expressway, "You Pay Nothing Unless We Get You a Settlement." In L.A., a family law practice advertisement shouts, "Get the Divorce Outcome You Deserve." Think *Better Call Saul.*

While it took some back and forth and a failed appeal, the United States Supreme Court eventually determined that "the disciplinary ruling serves to inhibit the free flow of commercial information and to keep the public in ignorance." By a narrow five to four decision, the Supreme Court agreed that John Bates and Van O'Steen had a right to advertise and, in so doing, fundamentally changed the way professional services firms go to market.

A Changing Landscape

With this decision, tectonic plates shifted the ground on which consulting and professional services stood. What was once illegal was now commonplace. Then technology began to flatten markets, the speed at which ideas were conceived and spread accelerated, and the number of consultants and professional service providers began to explode, roiling the marketplace for consulting and professional services and making it harder to sell those services. We all feel it. It seems harder to build our practice.

> Although repeat business and referrals still provide an important—and often the *most* important—source of new leads at many firms, they are no longer sufficient by themselves to sustain growth. During the halcyon days of flowing referrals, less competition, and simpler industry dynamics, many professional services firms operated less like a business and more like country clubs. Answer the phone was pretty much all the lead generation they did. Times certainly have changed.
> —Mike Schultz, John E. Doerr, and Lee W. Frederiksen, *Professional Services Marketing*

Specifically, four trends are making the sales of consulting and professional services more difficult:

The End of the Ban on Advertising

First, there is the Bates and O'Steen case. It cannot be overstated how profoundly this decision affected how consulting and professional services go to market. Prior to this ruling, marketing of consulting and professional services took place on the links or over drinks after work. Because the network was closed, it made sure prices stayed relatively high and uniform—a you-scratch-my-back-and-I'll-scratch-yours system. John and Van changed that. Today every accountant, architect, attorney, and web developer has a website, advertises, thinks about marketing and client development, and in general is less bashful about the need to think clearly about the process and costs associated with new client acquisition.

And this takes resources. A website, for example, is now table stakes—a requirement of a new business, not a choice. Marketing efforts have become something of an arms war. Staying afloat in the business means keeping up with what the competition is doing. It's not uncommon to overhear executives discussing the strategies of others in their field. "I heard they're doing a lot of white papers. I think we should as well." "They had David Cameron speak at their conference. Who should we get?" "You should see how they are all over social media. We don't even have a Twitter account."

The World Is Flat

Technology is flattening markets. The ability to phone, conference, email, collaborate, and browse regardless of where one lives allows companies to not just settle for the best expert in a local market but the best expert anywhere. This is transformative in that the net level of expertise in the world has gone up in proportion to how technology connects us.

This flattening of markets—call it the globalization of expertise—is a wonderful opportunity. Places like Madison, Wisconsin; Burlington, Vermont; Bozeman, Montana; Asheville, North Carolina; Portland, Maine; and Louisville, Kentucky all are home to sole practitioners and boutique firms whose practices are national and global. The number-one accountant for franchisors is in Des Moines, Iowa; the best ESOP attorney for services firms is in Santa Rosa, California; and the top outdoor products e-commerce web developer is in Grand Junction, Colorado. From the client's perspective, it makes no difference. Conference calls are conference calls. Indeed, it can be an advantage when a consultant or professional services provider lives in an expertise cluster because they are proximate to experienced talent and the newest ideas and innovation. For example, Toulouse, France, is known for its aerospace expertise, Copenhagen, Denmark, for its cleantech consultants, and Napa Valley for its wine production knowledge.

But globalization of expertise comes with a challenge. The larger (and noisier) a market, the harder it is for a buyer and seller to find one another.

If you live in a town of five thousand, you know the three realtors that serve the market. You see them at the supermarket, one of them has a kid who plays soccer with your kid, and one of them knows your husband from the town council. You know that one of the three realtors mostly focuses on commercial buildings. If you need to sell your house, you know to whom you should turn. If you have a downtown building you are interested in buying, you know who to go to. In a market like this, information flows efficiently. Buyers and sellers know each other and no barriers stand in the way of them trading with each other. Likewise, buyers of real estate in the market know where all the real estate is listed and can easily access that information.

The real estate market in New York, on the other hand, may be less efficient. A seller of a shopping center in the Bronx, for example, may not know of the best broker for that kind of property. She may know a handful of residential brokers, but they don't have good experience with shopping centers. One of those residential brokers, looking for referral fee, may recommend a commercial broker in Westchester, but that broker's knowledge of buyers in the Bronx may not be the best. It's possible our seller may find the absolute best representative for shopping centers in the Bronx by poking around, but it is equally possible that they do not.

We all feel the effects of this inefficiency. Tom was recently in New York sitting down with the management team of a regionalized IT consultant. This firm had considerable success in a number of cities and was now planting the flag in Manhattan. They rented trendy offices near the Flatiron Building outfitted with advertising agency–like décor, launched a website, and looked forlornly out the window at the skyscrapers. Suddenly, the idea of creating a beachhead for new business in the Big Apple seemed daunting. New York is *really big*, and it is hard to figure out where to start knocking on doors to build a practice. The group knew there was a niche they could fill, but none of their prospective customers knew they even existed. The complexity brought on by their new market, the very presence of twelve million people, hung around their necks like an anchor.

Firefly Ideas

A Firefly idea is one that lights up the room and then vanishes in an instant—big data, total quality management, IoT. One favorite trick of management consultants is to ask, "What are you doing on the data visualization front?" knowing full well that you are doing nothing, or better yet, have no idea what they are talking about. Your failure to have a cogent answer to their question allows them to do a gap analysis. "Why don't you fill out this questionnaire?" they ask. Then your answers magically metastasize into a project proposal.

Nothing new here, but it turns out that technology is accelerating the rate at which these ideas come and go. Researchers at the University of Louisiana, Lafayette studied sixteen management consulting "fashions" (their word and not ours) and found the average time that these concepts are hot is shrinking. In the 50s, 60s, and 70s, management ideas lasted a decade or more. In the 1990s, they lasted less than three years.

Today, management fashions go out of style in twelve or eighteen months at best.

If your ideas are your product and your product's shelf life is growing shorter, your marketing campaigns grow stale at the same rate. That makes it harder to keep your go-to-market materials current (not to mention the work involved in recasting yourself as relevant). Once, you could camp out on a good idea for a career. Now you have to reinvent yourself constantly.

More Players

The high prices and margins associated with expert services— compare a $250/hour HR consultant with a $40/hour assistant human resources professor—have caused the supply of consultants and professional services to go up. Professors are marching into consulting firms and volunteering to enlist in record numbers. Why wouldn't they? The pay is better.

At the same time, businesses are hiring more consultants and professional services providers as their business models shift from manufacturing to services and as they turn to so-called flexible workforces that depend on easily laid off contractors, a trend that has accelerated since Warren Wittreich first noted it in 1966.

> "In recent years, there has been a marked increase in the buying of professional services by management. This is true for a broad range of advisory activities, such as financial, economic, public relations, advertising, legal, personnel, research, and many others. By the same token, there has been a marked growth in the firms selling these services."
> —Warren J. Wittreich, "How to Buy/Sell Professional Services," *Harvard Business Review*, March/April 1966

The number of attorneys relative to the U.S. population remained steady for nearly one hundred years. Since 1970, however, the number of attorneys in the U.S. has more than tripled as a percentage of the population.

Similarly, the services industry as a whole has taken off over the last seventy-five years—especially when compared to the manufacturing sector. The gap between employment in the manufacturing and services sectors of the economy began to spread in the 1960s. The definition of "services" includes low-skill services like window washing—not just consulting and professional services—but we think it's safe to say the rise in consulting and professional services strongly correlates with that of the service sector as a whole. That means that there are a lot more people competing for your clients.

The Death of Scale

The venerable accounting firm Arthur Andersen, before it was sucked under by the toxic whirlpool called Enron in 2002, went to market as "one firm." Andersen never bought rival firms or hired anyone other than high-potential young people, which meant that all Andersenites around the world were hired, trained, and encultured at one facility in St. Charles, IL, about forty miles west of Chicago. But more than having a common vocabulary, parallel experiences, and a similar worldview, being an Andersenite meant being able to call any partner anywhere around the globe and pick their brain. What was good for you was good for a partner in London or Sydney. And there was a scale advantage to having this one firm in the marketplace. Andersen could credibly bid on the global audit work of a major transnational, confident that the staffing and expertise it brought to the table, regardless of geography, would be consistent and moving in the same direction.

Increasingly, however, the role of scale has diminished in the world of consulting and professional services. There's an advantage to having the attorney you hire to negotiate your employment contract be part of a global firm. If you are transferred to Johannesburg, they know the employment law there as well—but that can be offset by the expertise a sharply-niched provider brings to the table whether they are part of a big firm or working out of the guest bedroom as a sole practitioner. Combine this with the fact that the barriers to entry for consulting and professional services firms are falling, and scale does not always produce competitive advantage.

Technology obviates the need for a law firm to rent expensive downtown space next to the courthouse. At the same time, it has done away with the need for in-house law libraries and legal updates. Training is outsourced as is filing, billing, case financing, time tracking, and compliance. It used to be the walnut-sided conference room in a big law firm stood as evidence of the firm's ability to bring the resources necessary to successfully prosecute a case. Now it might just be seen as an indication of bloated overhead.

Obstacle #4: A Blizzard of Bad Advice

Everything You Know about Sales Is Wrong

We've absorbed through osmosis more than we might think about how to sell even if we have never taken formal coursework in the subject. It's a part of American pop culture captured in numerous books, plays, and movies over the generations: *Glengarry Glen Ross*, *Death of a Salesman*, *The Wolf of Wall Street*, *Margin Call*, and others. And that's a problem.

The fourth obstacle all of us face in trying to figure out a better way to build a bridge between us and potential clients is how *what we know about sales* is often wrong when it comes to consulting and professional services. The biggest challenge in our path to becoming a rainmaker may be actually unlearning what we think we already know.

Traditional Sales Training

Sales representatives in product-centered companies learn that sales is like a funnel. At the wide end of the funnel are prospective customers who are believed to be primed to buy our product. Leads are vetted, one-by-one, either in person, by phone or email, etc. The uninterested are culled, and the rest are pre-qualified into opportunities. This prequalification narrows the number of leads, which are then pitched and hopefully closed over time.

Hot Leads

Opportunities

Proposals / Quotes

New Customers

Traditional Sales Funnel

This funnel has dozens, or hundreds, of variations. The gist is always the same, however: sales is a numbers game based upon simple math:

Number of leads × yield rates = number of new accounts.

It is viewed by many sales organizations almost as a manufacturing process and managed similarly—with internal metrics, reports, and meetings. The sales funnel approach may be a useful approach for products with a high volume of prospective customers, but it's not terribly helpful when you are a credence good and when the entire universe of those you wish to serve may be represented by a few dozen organizations. When selling consulting or professional services, the goal is not to identify prospects and process them like corn flakes; *it is to identify a community and position yourself to serve it over time.*

The Science of Yield

When managing sales—either of oneself or others—the traditional sales funnel theory tells us to measure yield from one step to the next. If 20 percent of one hundred leads produce a first meeting, and half of those meetings lead to an opportunity to make a proposal, of which two eventually are sold, you have a 2 percent lead-to-sales yield. Pretty simple, really. The trick is to track and improve those yields over time.

This leads to the second half of how salespeople are taught to sell everything from railcar loads of coal to missile defense systems, namely, the tactics used to move from one step to the next. If improved tactics let you move your first meeting rate from 20 to 30 percent, you can increase your new accounts from two to three. It is just math.

So, and this is the question that sales trainers make their money on, how can you increase your yields? If you have ever been exposed to software, hardware, commodity, consumer product, or OEM sales, you've likely heard of Neil Rackham's SPIN selling, the consultative sale (they are largely the same), Miller and Heiman's Strategic Selling (the authors spun out of IBM to create their eponymous firm), Mike Bosworth's Solution Selling, Xerox's Needs Satisfaction Selling, or the Corporate Executive Board's Challenger Sale. All of these approaches are about how to choreograph moving from one level of the funnel to the next, generally from meeting to close, with the goal of improving yield. And, as we'll soon discuss, this array of sales techniques—while perhaps useful in selling mass-market consumer products—are not helpful at all in consulting and professional services. In fact, they may be more detrimental to our sales success than helpful.

A Rogues' Gallery of "Closing" Techniques

In his classic paean to cold coffee, stale cigarette smoke, and sales pits everywhere, David Mamet imagines a scene in the movie version of *Glengarry Glen Ross*, where Alec Baldwin plays a hotshot salesman from downtown who comes into a tired real estate sales operation to shake things up. He tells the worn-down men that their job is to sell. "Because only one thing counts in this life: get them to sign on the line which is dotted." It is simple, he says, "They are sitting out there waiting to give you their money. Are you going to take it?" The secret? The ABC's: "Always be closing."

Below is a list of "proven closing techniques." *We're not making this stuff up*. Maybe you have heard of a few of them, and some may have even been used on you the last time you bought a car:

- Alternative Close—offering a limited set of choices.
- Ask-the-Manager Close—use manager as authority.
- Assumptive Close—acting as if they are ready to decide.
- Balance-Sheet Close—adding up the pros and the cons.
- Best-Time Close—emphasize how now is the best time to buy.
- Bonus Close—offer delighter to clinch the deal.
- Bracket Close—make three offers, with the target in the middle.
- Calculator Close—use calculator to do discount.
- Calendar Close—put it in the diary.
- Companion Close—sell to the person with them.
- Compliment Close—flatter them into submission.
- Concession Close—give them a concession in exchange for the close.
- Conditional Close—link closure to resolving objections.
- Cost of Ownership Close—compare cost over time with competitors.
- Customer-Care Close—the customer care manager calls later and reopens the conversation.
- Daily Cost Close—reduce cost to daily amount.
- Embarrassment Close—make *not* buying embarrassing.
- Exclusivity Close—not everyone can buy this.
- Fire Sale Close—soiled goods, going cheap.
- Handover Close—someone else does the final close.
- Handshake Close—offer handshake to trigger automatic reciprocation.

- Hurry Close—go fast to keep them from thinking too much.
- IQ Close—say how this is for intelligent people.
- Minor Points Close—close first on the small things.
- Now-or-Never Close—to hurry things up.
- Opportunity Cost Close—show cost of not buying.
- Ownership Close—act as if they own what you are selling.
- Price-Promise Close—promise to meet any other price.
- Requirements Close—write down what they want as a formal requirement.
- Reversal Close—act as if you do not want them to buy the product.

(Excerpted from www.changingminds.org)

Sales managers have spent a lot of time chasing the grail of closing techniques that will increase the amount of sales their teams could bring home. We think this emphasis on technique misses the mark.

The Myth of the Perfect Pitch

A good friend of Doug's works for a successful midsized management consulting firm. Doug and his friend were having drinks one Friday after work, and his friend shared his senior partner's sales philosophy: "It's all about the pitch. You got to 'hook' them. If you don't have a compelling 'pitch,' you're dead in the water." If a prospective client didn't immediately 'bite' after his persuasive pitch, the senior partner's typical reaction was "Screw 'em! If they're too stupid to see the value in our proposal, then they're a bunch of idiots, and I don't want to work with them."

Both the question of how to hook a fish and how to land it depend on this emphasis on technique. If you take a sales training course, you will find that much time is spent thinking about and practicing these sorts of clever tactics.

This line of thinking goes: *if you could only prospect better, pitch better, negotiate better, and close better, you would win more business.* But that's not the typical way consulting and professional services are sold. We're sure if we took one of the negotiation programs offered in the in-flight magazines, we'd be much better at buying a home or car, but the fact is, being a master negotiator just isn't that relevant to earning trust and respect necessary to "close" a consulting or professional services assignment and might even be counterproductive. Great client relationships are built over time on foundations of trust and are not, by definition, transactional.

Better Personality

Sales trainers will also talk about polishing your personal skills, what we call the Better Personality approach, which was first popularized by Dale Carnegie in the 1930s with the runaway sales of his book, *How to Win Friends and Influence People.* The core of Carnegie's approach can be summed up as "It's possible to change other people's behavior by changing one's behavior toward them." The cover of the book promises to answer three questions:

1. What are the six ways of making people like you?
2. What are the twelve ways of winning people to your way of thinking?
3. What are the nine ways to change people without giving offense or arousing resentment?

A pleasant personality in and of itself isn't a bad thing, of course. The issue is that most individuals who have made it into consulting and professional services have already had the rough edges of their personalities sanded off. By the time they have finished law school or a top MBA program or made it to partner in their firm, most people are not lacking in people skills. It's not to say there aren't some who would benefit from a healthy dose of humility or empathy, but generally speaking, this isn't the limiting factor.

Sure, being likeable isn't a bad thing. It's just not typically the most important component of the credence buying decision. Respect trumps charm when it comes to most buying decisions for consulting and professional services. You'll frequently hear people say that "clients hire people that they like." We're not entirely convinced. If you are looking for a good bankruptcy attorney, do you focus more on whether they can protect your assets or would they be fun over drinks?

Why This Model Doesn't Work for Consulting and Professional Services

One of our core beliefs is that consulting and professional services are bought differently from products. They are bought on reputation, referral, and relationships—not on tangible features or attributes. They are credence goods, meaning their virtues cannot be tasted in advance of the sale; they must be bought on faith alone and that faith takes time to build.

Despite this, the temptation is to pretend the purchase of expert recruiting advice is the same as buying pork bellies in volume, and we can use the same funnel paradigm and step-by-step sales process to close a sales prospect.

But that's not true. Here's why:

The funnel assumes an infinite supply of leads. If you are selling accounting software for small businesses with up to $50 million in revenues, you can be pretty sure that a lifetime of pitching software will not exhaust the global supply of potential customers. On the other hand, if you sell predictive analytics to community, regional, and superregional banks in the United States, there are seven thousand potential customers (oh, and by the way, that is half the number there were fifty years ago). You'd be wise not to just churn and burn your way through such a relatively small list. If you design currency hedging strategies for reinsurance companies with a billion dollars (or more) in premiums written, you have thirty-seven potential clients. You might be thinking that's too small a market segment to serve, but you'd be wrong. Thousands of consultants and professional services practitioners "own" a similarly small segment, cover it up with a dominant service, and are compensated handsomely for their expertise. Look no farther than the "Big Four" accounting firms whose audit units are laser-focused on the Fortune 500, each with roughly 25% market share. With 125 audit clients, the addition of another dozen is material.

The funnel assumes that leads are of short duration. Read sales training advice for product salespeople, and it will tell you to read your prospect like a poker player might read her opponents. By closely observing what your potential customers say, you can determine if they are buyers, have objections that can be met, have objections that are a smokescreen for "real" objections, or are a "no," in which case, the best practice is to move on—no reason wasting time on a prospect who isn't going to buy. But that's not how it works in consulting and professional services. We've sat in on a Big Four partners meeting where their best rainmakers shared the advice they would give to young professionals. Said a senior partner,

Make friends on engagements when you are young, because the people you get to know at client companies will grow up and be decision makers. Stay in touch.

This is a decidedly different perspective—looking at a lead as a relationship to be cultivated over a lifetime. When the "financial advisors" in *Margin Call* were dialing the phone book to make a sale of their penny stocks, they didn't start over on a page when they got through with it. They were like sharks moving through the water—never stopping, never blinking, always swimming and looking for something new to eat. That might work for someone selling gym member-ships but not for those of us trying to engage with new clients. Successful practice leads in consulting and profes-sional services firms are much more like farmers cultivating their forty acres, careful with every relationship, knowing that if those relationships are treated well over time, they can sustain life.

The funnel assumes if you can measure, you should. Like the drunk who looks for his lost keys in the light below a street lamp and when asked why he is focused on such a small area, answers, "Because that's where I can see," there's an implicit choice being made by measuring yield just because it's available to measure. Maybe instead of measuring how many opportunities led to projects, a better measure would be "How deeply did you connect philosophically, intellectually, and socially with a key executive you met at a conference?"

That's not nearly as easy to measure as "What percentage of appointments did you set on those leads we purchased?" but it may be more strongly correlated with increased revenues per consultant over time.

The funnel fails to appreciate the referral effect. Doing good work for clients, staying in touch with them over time, having dinner and talking shop when you are in town, being helpful even when you are not under contract: These are the sorts of actions that deepen and maintain relationships. They are the throne on which positive word-of-mouth sits. You met a person who knew your sister-in-law. You dropped an email to your sister-in-law to say you met her friend, which reminds her that she just learned her son's soccer coach was in your business school, two years before you. She introduces you to the guy the next Saturday at practice when you stop by. You exchange small talk with him, but he begs off, saying he's headed to Singapore to a conference to speak. He leaves, and you check out his LinkedIn page on your phone. Turns out he speaks on how digital is transforming intellectual property management. You just received a letter from Paul Hastings saying they're abandoning their intellectual property practice, which has you on the hunt for a new IP attorney. You ping the guy asking for a referral. He says he knows a good sole practitioner who spun out of a large firm. Ten minutes later he writes you, saying he checked you out on LinkedIn while sitting at the gate and noticed you do work with manufacturing companies to outsource facility management. He has a client who just got a new CEO that is talking about focusing on core competencies. Would you be open to him introducing you to the head of manufacturing? What started as a guy you met on the soccer pitch turns into an introduction.

Here's the thing: every one of your new clients has a shaggy dog story like that. The typical funnel-based sales model doesn't appreciate shaggy dogs.

The funnel assumes the client's buying journey is linear. It assumes that you create awareness first, then uncover interest and desire, and finally catalyze action (this is the AIDA model of client engagement for those of you who took undergrad marketing). But what if you stumble on desire in a potential client *first*, like when a new acquaintance says he is looking for a website designer at a Friday-night cocktail party? That might cause you to follow up and say, "I'm a website designer" (awareness). In the process of designing his website (action), you lift the stone on what turns out to be his real problem, which is not the need for a website but the need for strategic focus (interest). Relationships for consultants and professional service providers almost never unfold serially. It is more like chords played on a guitar. Do you need to play the G chord in the second position before the D7 chord in the twelfth position in order to make music? No. You can, but it's also possible to enter a beautiful piece from the G chord first.

The funnel perpetuates the myth of the super-salesperson. By focusing on the meeting and the *art* of the sale, it suggests that some people have some special way with others that causes the target of their affection to bend to their wills. Like Svengali in George Du Maurier's novel *Trilby*, they are able to dominate and manipulate their subjects and cause them to do things they might not otherwise choose to. Not only is this creepy, it doesn't square with our experience. First, salespeople who are thought to be really good with people often come off as just inauthentic, oily, or unctuous. Call it the backfire effect. Second, we all know of experts who are just *terrible* with people but who have a line out the door. In consulting and professional services, substance matters, and experts who are known to be worth their weight in gold needn't be charmers. It's nice if they're nice, but nice isn't necessary.

How Clients Buy

8

The Secret to Selling

Never Say Sell

I actually don't think you can sell professional services. I think you
have to help clients buy them. Clients have problems and they need
help in discovering, understanding and tackling them. Once people
realize you helped them solve problems, then they will come back.
—Walt Shill, formerly of McKinsey and Accenture

A t 8:15 a.m. on Thursday, May 21, 2015, Sylvia Senaldi sent
an email to Dr. Peter Tyre:

Pete,
Meet Mac Shields. Mac attended your presentation recently
and wanted to see if you would be interested in meeting up
for coffee.

Mac is an old friend, a business associate and a smart guy. He has done great work for me in developing our go-to-market business strategy.

I'll let you guys take it from here!

Sylvia
Sent from my iPhone

Mac had heard Pete speak at a business conference the week before. He'd never heard of Pete's laser technology firm, LiDAR (basically radar with light waves instead of radio waves), before and found it fascinating. Also, Pete said something during his presentation that piqued Mac's interest: he was struggling to find a viable commercial opportunity for his firm's technology. Mac genuinely felt there was a real possibility that he could help Pete solve this business problem.

But Mac had never met Pete before. He looked him up on LinkedIn. There he saw that Pete was connected to his friend Sylvia, someone he had known for about twenty years. He asked Sylvia if she'd be willing to introduce them. Graciously, she said yes.

Pete's reply email came a few hours later that same morning:

----Original Message-----
From: Peter Tyre [mailto:tyre@peakphotonics.com]
Sent: Thursday, May 21, 2015 10:52 AM
To: Sylvia Senaldi; Mac Shields
Subject: Re: Intro

Thanks for the intro, Sylvia.

Mac, I'd love to meet up with you. I'm traveling until next Tuesday.
Do you have time next week before Friday?

Best regards,
Pete

Dr. Peter Tyre
Chief Executive Officer
Peak Photonics, Inc.

Mac admits that he has never been very good at cold calling. Actually, he hates it. Most people do—up there with fear of heights, spiders, and speaking in public. However, if it is someone he has a genuine interest in getting to know, Mac is happy to reach out. It helps if he has someone or something in common. A connection can make the outreach seem natural, sincere, and genuine; such was his interest in Pete's company and his mutual friend, Sylvia. In such cases, his approach didn't feel like cold calling or superficial networking; it felt more like making new friends.

Sylvia's email introduction was exceptional. Mac couldn't have scripted a better one if he had tried. Glowing client introductions like this one are tough to beat. With a solid introduction, the odds of getting a first meeting with someone are high.

Mac emailed Sylvia and Pete back later that same morning.

-----Original Message-----
From: Mac Shields [mailto:mac@shieldsassociates.net]
Sent: Thursday, May 21, 2015 11:11 AM
To: Peter Tyre; Sylvia Senaldi
Subject: Re: Intro

Yes, thanks for the introduction, Sylvia. Moving you to bcc:

Hi, Pete:
I enjoyed hearing you speak at the B2B Luncheon on Monday and learning a bit about Peak Photonics. I had

no idea there was such a cluster of photonics companies based here in Austin. I knew there were a few, but nothing to the level that exists today.

I'd like to take you to coffee, introduce myself and learn a bit more about Peak Photonics. Or, if it's more convenient to meet at your office, just let me know. How would next Thursday at 8:30 am work for you?

Thanks,
Mac Shields

Founder, Shields Associates, LLC.
mac@shieldsassociates.net
www.linkedin.com/in/macshields
www.shieldsassociates.net

Over the course of the summer of 2015, Mac and Pete developed a professional friendship. They met for coffee about once a month to talk about Peak Photonics, its technology, and the direction of the industry. Their coffee meetings had no real agenda. Mac was sincerely curious about Pete's technology and industry, and Pete, as a PhD physicist, was eager to pick Mac's brain on various business topics. Pete talked openly about the challenges he faced in finding compelling commercial opportunities for his company's technology. Mac shared a few ideas that he thought were relevant. He also sent him several articles and books he felt might be valuable.

After about six months and maybe a half-dozen meetings, Pete asked Mac if he would be willing to assist him with a project. Pete needed help developing a framework for analyzing new market opportunities. This was an area in which Mac had extensive expertise, and the topic also interested him. It felt to him that working with Pete would be a good collaboration. Mac wrote a proposal outlining his approach and the schedule and fees for the project. Pete accepted, and they started working together later that fall. A year after their first project was completed, Mac assisted Peak Photonics in analyzing a second emerging market opportunity.

Wouldn't it be great if more of our business development attempts felt so effortless?

Never Say Sell

No matter what euphemisms we use to describe the process of connecting with those we wish to serve—business development, client development, or sales and marketing—there remains the truth that *we need clients in order to be able to practice our professions*.

While many professionals shy away from the use of the word selling, it is clear that they work hard to win client work. We know we don't want to be selling, but we know doing nothing is not an option either. In her biography of Marvin Bower, Elizabeth Haas Edersheim reports,

> [He] worked hard at building the firm's reputation through-out his time at McKinsey. In 1939, he wrote several articles addressing organizational and financial issues with which U.S. companies were struggling at the time. He also made a dozen speeches at professional organizations, played count-less rounds of golf with prospective clients, lunched with executives at every opportunity, and encouraged everyone at McKinsey to do the same.

This may not be selling in the traditional sense, but Bower certainly wasn't sitting in his office waiting for the telephone to ring. How can we understand this in relation to selling and our aversion to all it represents? We need a new framework that can make sense of the work we must do to cultivate a network of clients to whom we can be helpful. The new discipline of design thinking can help.

Design Thinking Meets Business Development

Over the past two decades, there has been a renewed interest in the field of design. This renaissance was triggered in large part by the success of Apple's elegantly simple products designed by Jony Ive and brilliantly promoted by Steve Jobs. Herbert A. Simon, in his 1969 book *The Sciences of the Artificial*, first explored the notion of design as a "way of thinking" in the sciences. Since then, the term *design thinking* has become popular as a way to describe the mindset of a designer.

According to the cofounder of the Interaction Design Foundation (IDF), the Danish design think tank:

> Design Thinking is a design methodology that provides a solution-based approach to solving problems. It's extremely useful in tackling complex problems that are ill-defined or unknown by understanding the human needs involved and re-framing the problem in human-centric ways.
>
> —Rikki Dam, cofounder, IDF

For several decades, design thinking remained within the world of design. Beginning in the early 1990s, others in the field of design observed that the approach could be useful for problem solving in a broader context. David Kelley, in particular, was highly influential in bringing the design thinking philosophy to the challenges of solving business problems.

Kelley is as close as it gets to being a rock star in the world of design; he's both the cofounder of IDEO (the international design and consulting firm based in Palo Alto, California) and Stanford

University's Hasso Plattner Institute of Design (known as the d. school). David earned an undergraduate degree in electrical engineering from Carnegie Mellon, but he later admitted that "it didn't feel quite right." Fortunately for us, his early work at Boeing sparked an interest in the study of design, and in the mid-1970s, he returned to school and earned a master's degree from Stanford University's product design program.

David says, "The main tenet of design thinking is empathy for the people you're trying to design for."

The principles of design thinking are now being used in corporations beyond the traditional scope of product design. According to Jon Kolko in the article, "Design Thinking Comes of Age," in the September 2015 issue of the *Harvard Business Review*:

> There's a shift under way in large organizations, one that puts design much closer to the center of the enterprise. But the shift isn't about aesthetics. It's about applying the principles of design to the way people work.

Simply put, design theory implores us to examine a customer's (or client's or user's) experience and reverse engineer how to make that experience better. This may sound obvious, but what Kelley and others saw when they looked at product design was that much of design started from the needs of the designers or the constraints of manufacturing instead of the end user.

That rang a bell for us. Traditional sales training emphasizes what the salesperson should do—generate leads, prequalify them and then meet, persuade, and close clients. But maybe that is all wrong. Maybe we should not all be asking, "what should sales-people do?" but rather, "*how do clients buy?*"

Using a design-thinking mindset, we started asking ourselves questions that focused on exploring the client's experience.

- How do prospective clients think when hiring us?
- What are a client's buying criteria?
- How do clients choose between alternative service providers?
- How do others in the organization influence the decision-making process?
- How does a client decide that the timing is right to hire us?
- How does a client evaluate our performance?
- How does a client decide if they will hire us again in the future?
- Are there similarities in the way clients think about the various professional services?

Answering these questions helped us identify seven elements that provide a pragmatic framework for better understanding how clients buy. These seven elements represent the steps that a prospective client moves through when deciding to hire you.

The seven elements of the client's journey are:

1. I am **aware** of you and/or your company.
2. I **understand** what you do and how you and your firm are unique.
3. I have an **interest** in what you do because it is relevant and potentially of value to me.
4. I **respect** your professional expertise and believe that you can help me.
5. I **trust** that you are honest. I believe you have my best interest at heart, and I feel comfortable working with you.
6. I have the funds and organizational support and have the **ability** to buy from you.
7. This is a priority for me, and I am **ready** to engage.

FIGURE 8.1 The Seven Elements of the Client's Decision Journey

These steps may occur sequentially, but they don't have to. Prospective customers can be aware of you and understand exactly what you do. They can respect you and trust you. But until there is a genuine need, organizational support, and funding, they aren't interested, able, or ready. Some services are triggered by specific events. Until that time comes, your help isn't required. For example, the need for the services of an estate or tax attorney may be triggered by the death of a loved one. Or the services of an architect may be required when a couple becomes "empty nesters" and decides to build a smaller home.

The Consultant Becomes the Client

Arthur Chung has been both a consultant, two or three years from making partner at A.T. Kearney, and a client—when he left A.T. Kearney to lead Google's Global Retail Launch Strategy group. He remembers business development at ATK.

> We'd identify clients we wanted to work with and strategize about how we would get our foot in the door, each of us taking on different tasks. We hunted in packs. I remember worrying about how I would do business development on my own. I couldn't see making a bunch of cold calls.

If only Arthur knew then what he knows now that he is at Google and has consultants begging to work with him. If only Arthur knew how clients actually buy.

From his perch on the Google campus in Mountain View, the world looks very different from when he was a consultant. "There are many companies that come in and solicit us. Our workdays are very full; we are juggling thousands of leads. We're always thinking about time. To prune and talk only to companies we think can add value, we generally only talk to people we have worked with before. Every lead has someone here attached to it. Someone calls me and says, 'I used to work with this team and I think they might have a unique perspective.' When the partner in the firm reaches out, I'll talk with them. But there is always a connection."

Arthur never talks about "need," particularly. Instead he is looking to partner with smart people.

> The consulting firms that don't do their homework fail miserably. There are lots of consulting companies that have retail experience. When they don't do their homework to understand what we've done in retail already, it's an immediate turnoff. We'll ask questions early on to understand if they even know our landscape or if they are making vague references to what we've done. I remember one particular firm I was impressed with. They actually went out to retail stores and some of our competitors and had developed a point of view. It wasn't necessarily 80% right, more like 50%, but still it showed they had invested some time. Those that work a little harder and have developed a unique point of view I care about. They get my attention.

> Here's the thing. Clients want to buy. They have business objectives they hope to achieve. They have resources and are scouring the world to find people who they can trust and who can add value. But they buy in a very particular way.

David Kelley's brother and general manager of IDEO, Tom Kelley, tells a wonderful story about a project IDEO took on. Oral-B sold electronic toothbrushes and for a while owned the market. Then, as competitors came in, they began to lose market share. They hired IDEO to help design the next generation of children's toothbrushes. IDEO started by looking at kids brushing their teeth. What they found fairly quickly was that kids lacked the kind of basic dexterity needed to hold and manipulate a normal toothbrush. The handle was too thin. IDEO began to experiment with fat-handled toothbrushes. Kids loved them, and a new product was born: the Squish Gripper.

Let's do the same thing. We think it will help change the way we think about selling.

9

Element 1: I Am Aware of You

What Was the Name of Your Firm Again?

A s Oscar Wilde wrote in *The Picture of Dorian Gray*, "there is only one thing in the world worse than being talked about and that is not being talked about." It's one of the most basic truths in commerce: if a prospective client doesn't know you exist, they cannot buy from you.

The entire sales and marketing profession sits atop this little gem of obviousness. Broadcast advertising, sales reps, Internet advertising, direct mail, public relations, content marketing, email campaigns, search engine optimization (SEO), trade shows, social media, and event marketing are all arrayed in front of business people for them to choose among, like bracelets in a jewelry store.

Of course, these tactics do other work as well—explaining what you do and why it makes sense to engage with you—but one of the first jobs of marketing is to let others know who you are. Absent this knowledge, you don't exist. The threshold work of sales and marketing is to cause your name to pass through the minds of those you most want to serve.

Why? Because prospective clients cannot engage with us unless they know us. The great handshake that is commerce starts with an introduction. Your client cannot choose you unless she or he knows your name.

To a Land Where You Are Not Known

Forty years ago, a young man sat in a small rural classroom located 193 kilometers east of Vancouver on the Trans-Canada highway and hung on his teacher's every word.

> The teacher who inspired me most was Miss Stubson from my high school in Sardis. She was phenomenal because she raised everyone's aspirations. She used to drive in from Vancouver, from the 'big city' to teach in this school no one had heard of. She'd say: "you can do a lot in the world—go for it!" At thirteen or fourteen, she opened my horizons. And she was pushy about it. She started up a debating society, which the school had never had, and then entered us for the regional championships, then the provincial, then the national. She said: "You need to do more than just school work. Debating is going to develop you. And anyhow, I've already entered you—you're going!"

The young man in Miss Stubson's class took these words to heart, graduating from the University of British Columbia with honors and then winning a Rhodes scholarship to Brasenose College at Oxford University. After a stint working as a currency analyst for Rothschild, he took a position in the Toronto office of a consulting firm.

> I figured I'd come for two years and get as much experience as I could, then go back to the academic world. The more I worked in the firm, however, the more curious I grew. You're always learning. Just as soon as you get comfortable with something, you go to the next level, and I love that.

The years passed. He enjoyed his work, was climbing the consulting ladder, enjoyed the respect of his colleagues, and was comfortable, increasingly ensconced in the Toronto business community. That's when the Toronto office nominated him to join the international partnership, but after interviewing, he failed to make the cut. It was devastating for someone who was so used to succeeding.

> It took me three times before I was elected a partner. It was a very painful process. . . . I hadn't experienced a lot of failure. I had worked hard, and you know, if you work hard, you do well. Here I was. I was working hard and I was rejected.

The interviews were tough. "One of them was very painful. [The reviewer said,] 'we're not sure about your problem-solving skills.' That's like telling an astronomer they can't do math. It was a bit of a slap in the head."

When an opportunity to work for the firm in Korea came up, he jumped even though everyone around him advised him not to go. "You're going to kill you career," they said, but it didn't deter him. He said to himself, "I am going to go. I'm going to be tested like I've never been tested. I'll learn some things. And if it doesn't work out, I can live with that. But I know I'm going to grow."

> When I moved to Korea, I had nothing. I didn't know the language, [and] I didn't know the culture. I didn't know any people. I had nothing. And that is kind of why I wanted to go because I wanted to try and figure it out.

And Dominic Barton did figure it out. He built a robust banking practice for McKinsey & Co. in South Korea, and even became friends with the president. Then, on the strength of that success, he was asked by McKinsey to lead the firm's Asia practice based in Shanghai. He became known for his vision, drive, intelligence, and strong commitment to the values of the firm. In 2009, his fellow senior partners from around the world elected him to be the firm's eleventh global managing director. He was forty-six years old.

Introducing Yourself

When Dominic first landed in South Korea, he knew he needed to introduce himself to the business community. He carried with him the halo of the McKinsey brand, to be sure, but that didn't take away from the fact that he was an outsider to the clubby world of Seoul banking.

> I asked people for help. I wrote ten letters to banking CEOs. I didn't say, "Look, I'm Dominic Barton from McKinsey. I'm here to help." It was, "I've moved here, I want to help play a small role in building the financial system, but I don't know anyone. All I have is my experience from x, y, and z. Can I get some advice from you? Would you help me?" Some of my colleagues were a bit shocked that I would write a cold letter

because that's not sort of done, but nine out of the ten CEOs wrote me back. 'Sure, come and talk,' they said. But I wasn't writing to do work. I was writing to ask for help. That is how I established a network. People would refer me to other people. I got to know people. I didn't have any other natural linkage.

Interviewing for information in this way is enormously effective. Think about the advice you might give your younger self if you had recently graduated from college and were looking for a job.

"I love fishing and hiking, and I'd like to work in the outdoor products industry."

You might ponder your younger self and say, "You can troll websites for job openings, or you can send a cold letter requesting employment, but it would be better to network in the industry. Many jobs are created for individuals or are not widely advertised."

"How do I network?"

"You use introductions and politely written inquiries to ask people's advice, both on your job hunt and to get their perspective on where the industry is headed. At the end of each interview, ask if there are others with whom you should be talking and if the person minds if you use their name when reaching out to others."

This is job hunting 101. It is no different in consulting and professional services.

Note a few lessons from Dominic's experience:

Intentions matter. Dominic did not do sales-like things, like leave a white paper or talk about a new service offering, because he knew he was not selling; he was learning. To his mind, it would be impossible to be of service to an industry or geography without understanding the context into which he was walking. His desire to introduce himself to the financial services industry in Seoul was genuine, but so was his desire to hear the perspective of those who most wanted to serve.

Values matter. Marvin Bower created a firm in which the value of service was higher than the value of growth or firm profit. It's not that those things are not important; it's that the value of impartial advice given to clients was more important than commercial success. That means that at the margin, you always make the call in favor of the client and truth and away from self-interest. There's a kind of belief in karmic business going on here: Do the right thing and it will return to you in ways you cannot predict.

Time matters. Dominic did not seek to sell right as he landed at Incheon International Airport. His highest priority was to serve. From that came a desire to introduce himself and to learn. Consulting is service, and service begins with knowing those you hope to serve. In aggregate, this becomes your network. Russell Davis at BCG reports that the advice given to new hires is "do good work and build your network." That's because networks are people sitting in various institutions and with various titles who have overlapping interests and who bring different skills to the table. Work—in the sense of consulting and professional services engagements—are handshakes between nodes in that network agreeing to join their complementary skills and experiences together on projects. This engagement rarely happens after a first meeting. Instead trust and reputation are built up over time, like clouds thickening over the ocean. One day there will be an opportunity to collaborate, but wishing the rain would come sooner does not make it so.

A second approach that Dominic took was to write and give speeches.

> I had a weekly column in a kind of business newspaper. I
> would also agree to give speeches to anyone who wanted me
> to speak, but I had a rule that I had to meet the CEO before
> the speech and afterwards to understand the context of what
> was going on and to follow up.

Again, Dominic takes the view that his job is to participate in and support the conversation going on in his industry. It is a long view that says, *"Give value first, build and support the network, and the rest will follow."*

The Awareness Trap

For most of us, when we think about building awareness for our firms and our practices, we grow queasy, thinking, "Our firm has just fifty consultants. There's no way we can put billboards in the airport like Deloitte or Accenture."

And, of course, this is true. You can't spend millions to build your name recognition, but it's a trap to think this is the only way to build awareness or that such scale would even be helpful. Too often, we equate awareness with mass advertising and in so doing falsely liken the kind of awareness appropriate to a consulting or professional services practice to the kind of awareness appropriate to consumer products.

The business models serving consumer products and expert services are very different, and what works for one, is wholly inappropriate for the other. In consumer products, advertising is the only way to reach customers efficiently because you need so many of them. With profits on soap measured in pennies, millions of customers are needed. But just as you would never think about sitting down with a customer one-on-one if you were a Colgate-Palmolive executive trying to sell more Irish Spring, if you are a sole proprietor, it makes no sense to broadcast advertise.

> I think reputational advertising and branding, the tradi-tional branding, where you spend a lot of money and create an image, is much less effective in this space, because at the end of the day, that may create name awareness but it doesn't create preference or even understanding of what you do, until you actually sit down face-to-face with folks and talk about what people you might bring to them and how those people might solve their particular problems. So, while it creates a general awareness of who we are, com-pared to selling a product, I can't do very much with advertising to create an image, or create differentiation that makes people want to buy Navigant the same way they might want to buy an iPhone 7.
> —Ed Keller, Chief Marketing Officer, Navigant Consulting

This is just to say that in thinking about how a potential client becomes aware of us, it pays to remember that there are approaches, like picking up the phone or shooting someone an email, that are likely to be more cost-effective, and simply more effective, than hanging a banner in Times Square.

200 People You Need to Know

The question then becomes, *how do you build your brand awareness*? More specifically, how do you:

- Figure out with whom you should be speaking?
- Find the time to introduce yourself to all of them?

The good news is the number of people who might potentially engage with you is smaller than you think. Our view is that there are roughly two hundred people who make all the difference in your world. If you offer economic analysis for law firms, there are two hundred litigators who, if they knew who you were and used you on their cases, would keep you busy for the rest of your life. If you are an architect at a large New York firm that builds skyscrapers around the world, there are two hundred developers who need to know your name.

Two hundred might not be the right number for your business, but it's not five million.

Dominic's number is five hundred.

> I think there's a number of ways you can stay in touch with people without it being obtrusive. One way I do it is that I sort of feel I'm reading for about five hundred people. When I read something in the media, or I read a book, or I come across an interesting conversation, I go out in my mind's eye to these five hundred people. I'm making up the number, but it's that order of magnitude. They are people I've known. Then if I see something, I'll just get it to my assistant and say, "Can you please send a copy of this to. . . ." I also think that these five hundred or so people, they are reading for me, that they will send me something when they see it and think of me.

Once you wrap your head around this notion of narrowcasting, building awareness becomes much more straightforward and decidedly less expensive.

The Lost Art of the Cold Call

The Blue Devils were down. Duke would either advance to the Final Four or get washed out of March Madness. With less than a minute to go, they hit a three-point shot and were up again. The crowd went crazy. Stephanie Cole and her husband Dave were at home on the edge of the sofa shouting at the TV. Neither were Duke fans, but both had Duke winning. The path to a winning bracket seemed much more in reach.

Suddenly, Stephanie, a managing director at PIE, the firm Tom runs, remembered the LinkedIn profile of an executive she'd been trying to meet. "I knew we could help him, so I had decided to cold call him." She'd left voicemails and sent occasional emails for more than a year, but he had been unresponsive. Now as students rushed the floor after the final buzzer, she turned to Dave and said, "he's a Blue Devil."

The next morning, she pinged the executive and congratulated him on the win. "That's the key to cold calling. Try to find something in common with the person you are calling." The executive got right back to Stephanie.

In an age when computers are ubiquitous, it is easy to want to automate the selling of expert services. Software can have its place, but nothing replaces human contact. If you see someone you feel you can help, sometimes it makes sense to just pick up the phone.

Let's be clear here: phoning someone you do not know can be scary. We would much rather publish a white paper on a subject and hope that customers beat a path to our door, but to rely on that as your only means for making new friends is crazy. Overcome the fear, find the phone number, and make the call—resolute in your belief that your experience can complement the experience of the person you are calling, and that together there is a least the possibility of creating value that each of you could not create alone.

Stephanie has a method to the lost art of the call:

- Develop a thesis: What companies can you potentially help with your expert services?
- Identify the role: Inside the company, what is the function you would be helping?
- Find the person: Call into the switchboard or search online. Identify the name of the person you are trying to reach.
- Make the call: Leave a voicemail for the person you are trying to reach. Most people don't pick up their phones these days. Your job is to communicate that you are a human being and not a robot. Don't sound too polished. Cold calling is not your full-time job. Tell them you must have missed them and that you will send an email.
- Find their email: Look online. Look for email patterns in a company. Don't be afraid to send several different email combos in the hope that one hits.
- Keep your email short and ask for a call: Reference your voicemail. Try to reference something personal or points of intersection. Research what is happening in their lives or their companies. Don't get carried away, though. Research can be a way to put off the call.
- Double-check your email: This is your first impression. It is worth a second read before you press "send."
- Follow through: The people you are trying to reach are very busy, but what they have no time for today, they may have time for tomorrow.

Tactics—What Works

Here is how to build awareness for your service offering:

- **Ask for advice.** We've learned that simply asking for advice on your practice can be monstrously successful at getting your name out. Let go of this idea that you have to be the smartest person in the room.

- **Publish your point of view.** Whether you blog, podcast, write articles, white papers, or books, writing and podcasts announce to the world your interest in a domain. A few rules: Stick to your segment. Focus is your friend. You want to be known as a dominant and consistent voice in your industry. Have a practice doing audits for large agricultural cooperatives? Stay away from commenting on the rise of low-cost steel flooding U.S. markets. Second, do not feel you need to be the expert. This is hard to swallow for people who make their living selling expertise. Here's the truth, though: You get as much credit by bringing together those who are inventing the answers in various companies as you do by being a would-be font of knowledge. Third, learn how content can be published (in a trade journal) and then republished (via a Twitter feed or broken up into LinkedIn posts).

- **Speak.** Increasingly, speaking berths at industry conferences are awarded to those who sponsor the conferences. This pay-to-play reality seems a vaguely wrong way for conference providers to act. You'd think they would be mostly interested in "publishing" the best content, not just the featured articles of those who are paying the freight, but that's the world we live in. Exceptions are made for keynotes and authors. There's nothing better than a speech in front of exactly the right target audience to at least give you the opportunity to shine and impress. We say, "at least," because not everyone is a speaker, and it is best not to pretend you are if you are not.

- **Host summits.** All large consulting and professional services firms sponsor summits of various sorts. This can be a dinner in Manhattan or a three-day affair in Amsterdam. The standard format is to invite clients and would-be clients to travel to the event, which might feature panel discussions, notable industry speakers, and one-on-ones with partners offsite. These events are very effective at husbanding hard-won relationships. A caveat, though. Our experience is that summits are not very good at attracting people you do not already know. It all starts out innocently enough. Your marketing director says, "You have a growing education practice. Let's throw an event where we invite college and university chief administrative officers. We can do it in Orlando." Suddenly the budget is $200,000, which might make sense if you got 200 potential clients to attend, but then the responses to the "Save-the-Date" you sent out come back, and the numbers look soft, with most of registrants already being clients.

- **Attend conferences.** Go to an industry conference and meet people you don't now know. In an effort to maximize exposure, some firms sponsor dinners (again, the danger is you are taking out your existing clients, which is not bad, but not the same as getting your name out there), underwrite substantive panels (how much is that placard worth on the dais?), attend cocktail events (make sure you don't hang out with your friends), or host tradeshow booths (Johnson and Smith—Accountants to the Gaming Industry!) along with offering collateral materials and free giveaways. A better practice is to ignore much of the conference and set up coffees beforehand with the fifteen people you want to get to know or to sponsor a best-practices roundtable offsite for invited guests. Remember the point is not to have everyone at the conference know your name. Stay focused on your list of two hundred. A single coffee with the CFO of a target company is worth five thousand refrigerator magnets with your name on it handed out at a booth.

- **Write emails.** Writing emails to specific people with specific, well-researched requests for time yields results. The key is follow-up.

- **Host best practice roundtables.** Tom's company, PIE, builds groups of potential clients on behalf of consulting and professional services firms. The executives talk about best practices, and the client firms get to make new friends in a substantive environment as hosts of the calls. Because what is asked of executives is low (one-hour phone call with peers, not a webinar), participation is high and the method has proven to be an effective way for expert service providers to make new friends.

- **Write newsletters.** For many years, Walt Shill, the former head of North American consulting for Accenture, wrote *Friday Thoughts*, a simple email where he told a story or two and tried to add value by reflecting on them. He had a wonderful style of writing, and his mailing list quickly grew into the thousands. Many of us looked forward to reading what was essentially a proto-blog using the one-to-many technology of an email list, and it certainly kept him on the top of people's minds and served as a calling card to the many who received forwarded copies of individual pieces. Twitter and Medium would have made his life easier, but the effect would have been largely the same.

In the end, there's not one right or best approach; there are only approaches executed with heart. "I think everyone has their own model of how they do it. I think you have to figure out the approach you are most comfortable with," says Dominic.

The difficulty is not choosing the right tactic; it's having the discipline to stick with an approach that is appropriate to who you are over time. We have all seen professionals among us dart about chasing the latest marketing fads. Doug calls this approach the Unicorn Quest. One month they're all about upgrading their website; after that it's search engine optimization. Then they try an email newsletter and after that run some ads in a trade journal. Someone says podcasting is the future, so they give that a try, and then the next month they're off to the latest trade show. Before long, they're on a mission to land a speaking gig.

This Unicorn Quest can work, at least some of the time. We all get lucky occasionally and stumble into a client. A better approach, though, to building awareness is to find the two or three of these tactics that fit your personal style and stick with them over a long period of time. You don't need to use all of the tactics, just a few. None of these are get-rich-quick schemes but are instead proven ways to underwrite a community and its conversation over time in a way that positions you to be of help if it is needed.

The Myth of Marketing Automation

Marketing automation is software used to streamline sales and marketing by replacing high-touch, repetitive manual processes with automated solutions. Whether or not you realize it, you've been on the receiving end of marketing automation. It's responsible for the mass of email content you get from companies or brands to which you have given your contact information to.

Many mid-to-large consulting and professional services firms are currently implementing or thinking of implementing marketing automation software such as Marketo, Hubspot, and Pardot. It's white hot at the moment. Many in our industry have been sold on the promise of marketing automation generating volumes of new qualified leads and inbound customer interest. Unfortunately, in our opinion, the promise is much greater than the reality for those in consulting and professional services.

Here's how it works: Every purchase or event or subscription you have been a part of collects your contact information and then blasts you with subsequent messages. Software tracks your actions and sends you more stuff (content) that the company thinks you will be interested in: news and announcements, articles, new product releases, and sales promotions. You may even get a phone call from a live salesperson. If you click on messages or download information, the software refers your contact information to a practice head on a list of what it describes as qualified leads. The question is, are those qualified leads? Does interest in a subject correlate with the ability to buy? Secondly, note that the software quickly volleys the next step back to you. When you receive the list, it is incumbent upon you to pick up the phone and talk with the "lead." Our question is, if you know the two hundred people in companies who, if they were buyers, would turbo-charge your growth, why not just pick up the phone in the first place and leave the software out of it?

Before we get tarred with bad-mouthing marketing automation, let us say that it can be highly effective for certain industries—for example, consumer products where it is a useful way to automate high-volume digital communication tasks. Our issue is the application of marketing automation to consulting and professional services. In our fields, we typically have dozens or hundreds of prospective clients, not tens of thousands or a million.

Do we really need to automate a stream of digital content when we're trying to reach a relatively small group of people in a personalized way? Why not use snail mail to share a hard copy of your latest white paper complete with a handwritten note with a dozen prospective clients? Follow this up with a phone call a week later inviting your friend to a moderated round table discussion on the topic, or coffee or dinner to discuss their thoughts.

10

Element 2: I Understand What You Do

You Do What?

Prospective clients may have heard of you but it is possible they still have no idea what you do. To complete the handshake, would-be clients must clearly understand exactly what you do, who you serve, and how you are unique.

Once, professional services firms were called names like "Garcia Tax Preparation," or "Hanson's Staffing," but now with the rise of vaguely Latinate, abstract names like "Amised" or "Infomax," all bets are off on understanding what a firm does from its name. A possible client—someone who would benefit from your expertise—might drive past your gleaming office building, the one with the six-foot-high illuminated sign, for sixteen years straight and *have no idea what you do* if your name is something generic.

> If people recognize the name of your firm but don't understand what you do or who you do it for, the name recognition is of little value.
> —Mike Schultz, John E. Doerr, and Lee W. Frederiksen,
> *Professional Services Marketing*

Lessons from 55 BC

For Cicero, one of Rome's most famous orators, rhetoric included five canons: invention, arrangement, style, memory, and delivery. His *De oratore* contained practical advice on each. To improve one's memory, he counseled using the method of loci. He illustrated the device by retelling the famous story of Simonides of Ceos.

Simonides was a poet who made his living composing lyric poems for noblemen whose idea of fun was to eat roasted goat, drink red wine, and listen to raconteurs wax on about their virtues in front of their friends. One evening, Simonides was performing for one client, a man called Scopas. The man must have been an undistinguished sort, because Simonides ran out of material halfway through the performance. Knowing he had a time slot to fill, he turned his praise to the twin gods, Castor and Pollux. His thought was that by talking about the two gods, it would elevate his client Scopas by association.

As the evening drew to a close, Simonides took a bow only to have Scopas stand and wag his finger. "I'll not pay for this," he thundered. "It wasn't about me. It was about the gods."

Simonides stood frozen. Only after a minute of silence did he manage to say, "I tried to sing of your handsomeness and good wisdom . . . ."

"I am a fair man. I'll pay for half the poem. Get your gods to pay the other half."

The room exploded in drunken laughter at Scopas' cleverness, and Simonides began to relax. Not his most profitable night, but at least he hadn't been beaten or worse.

Just as he was packing to leave, a messenger ran into the hall and whispered something in Simonides' ear. Two men apparently were asking for him outside. Simonides begged leave, walked out to the patio, and looked around for the men but couldn't find them when suddenly, he felt the earth under his feet shake. A line of potted plants toppled over and crashed on the tiled floor. Then the entire house shook and collapsed on itself.

Servants and neighbors came running to help, but there was nothing to be done. The dead, including Scopas and his friends, lay mangled under heavy building stones. Relatives filed in to locate their loved ones, but were unable to identify the bodies. Simonides was called to help. He looked at the mass of rubble and then remembered the table and who was sitting where. It had been Atticus at the left, Cassius next, with Scopas in the middle. Soon he had the bodies sorted.

Cicero called this mnemonic the method of loci—the method of places. He said to remember a series of facts or statements, place the chain of items in a series of imagined places. It makes remembering them easier.

To this day the method of loci is used by world champion memory competitors. Clemons Mayer used this method to memorize more than one thousand numbers in half an hour at the memory half-marathon. He constructed a mental trail around his home with three-hundred stops and "stored" numbers in each spot. To recall them, he thought about the series of places and the numbers came back to him. Ed Cooke, another memory competitor, describes how he thinks of crazy places—he says *the odder the better*—like parts of his dog's sleeping cushion. Once he has the sequence of places down in his head, he can remember anything he wants by associating what he wants to remember with the different places.

Endel Tulving, a native of Estonia, emigrated to Toronto after World War II, escaping the annexation of Estonia by the Soviets. There he studied experimental psychology and eventually earned a doctorate from Harvard.

Tulving liked to demonstrate to his students that memories exist even if we cannot recall them. He'd shout out a random list of words—pencil, cloud, clock, run, yellow, rotten, fever—in rapid fire. Then he'd ask his students to write down the words they could remember. If he said twenty words, the best in the group would get ten. Then he'd ask the students if the words they couldn't remember were lost forever? Most thought they were. To which he would turn to a student and say, "What was the color on the list?" Inevitably, they would smile and say "yellow."

Tulving believed that memories lived in boxes, but in order to retrieve those boxes, you had to have an access route to get to them. He and his research assistant designed a large-scale memory test and found that unaided, participants could recall 45 percent of a list, but if you cued them by asking them not just to recall anything that was on the list but a specific item—like what the color or writing utensil was on the list—*the success rate jumped to 75 percent.*

How Clients Remember You

The typical consumer is overwhelmed by unwanted advertising, and has a natural tendency to discard all information that does not immediately find an empty slot in his mind.
—Al Ries and Jack Trout, *Positioning*

When do you think Ries and Trout made this claim? 2015? 2010? 2000? 1990? Would you believe 1969? Even before smartphones, the Internet, email, social media, or the 24/7 news cycle, they saw we were already overwhelmed with too much noise. Fast forward fifty years. Consumers feel besieged by an unrelenting onslaught of advertising messages.

When Al Ries and Jack Trout first made this claim, the average American consumer was exposed to about five hundred ads a day. By the early 2000s, this number had grown to an estimated five thousand ad messages a day. Today, marketing experts estimate that many among us are exposed to as many as ten thousand ads a day. Ries and Trout remind us that our brains hurt at five hundred. At some point, advertising becomes meaningless, or worse, background noise.

With this blizzard of information swirling around us, most of it is discarded as useless. But we do remember the pieces of information that are relevant, which we store away by putting them into mental houses that can be cued and recalled.

Clients Have to Understand Who You Are

In order for clients to buy from you, not only do they have to be aware you exist, but they also have to have a good sense of what you do. If they don't, they can't build a bridge from you to the problem they have now or might face in the future. Put another way, they won't remember you because you don't live in a box that has a strong access route to it. They aren't associated with a "place" in Cicero's words.

We have found that consulting and professional service providers who are well known to the world they want to impress do two simple things:

- They niche themselves and become known for that niche.
- They articulate *what they do, who they serve, and how they're unique* in a short, pithy sentence—the so-called "elevator pitch."

Do these two things well, and people will not only understand what you do, but they will remember you later when they need help or when someone asks them for a recommendation on who is the expert in a field.

Patrick Pitman is the founder of E-Business Coach, an Austin-based digital consultancy that specializes in building e-commerce platforms for businesses. Patrick discovered early on in his career the value of specialization.

> When there's a really clear association in your mind between a person that you trust and the problem that they can solve, it makes it easier to refer you. For the longest time, my business was based primarily on referrals. Referrals happen when there is a clear association in someone's mind. When they come across a problem, your name comes to mind. So, I think that specialization is important because specialization is where referrals come from.

To successfully niche, understand there are metacategories that we carry around all the time. They are "first," "best," and "biggest."

> Who is the *biggest* cola company? Coca-Cola.
> Who is the fifth-biggest cola company? Don't know.
> Who was the *first* president? George Washington.
> Who was the twenty-first president? Don't know.
> Who is the *best* online retailer of shoes? Zappos.
> Who is the ninth-best online shoe retailer in the United States? Don't know.

It is as if without knowing it, we are subconsciously memorizing vast amounts of random pieces of information by following Cicero and Tulving's advice. We can recount Coca-Cola's name because it lives in a room. Recall the room—a room called "the largest"—and Coca-Cola's name floats to the surface of our mind's vast pond.

This sounds easy, but it is not. Kris Klein, the founder and managing partner of Lenati, a marketing and sales strategy consultancy based in Seattle, says:

> The first thing in selling consulting services is to create a point of differentiation. But not to be so different that people don't understand what you do. We played around for a while with the idea that, "Gosh, we needed to create a new market. We need to create something new." We were so small that we needed to be different than everybody else in the market in order to create a point of differentiation. And the reality is, that was a huge mistake. We failed miserably trying to do that. Our language was dissonant to people. They couldn't understand what we were doing well: we clearly weren't articulating it well. And they struggled to find a moment to buy.

To niche ourselves, we need to decide what we are good at and then define it—by geography, company size, or another quantifier—and then practice a succinct pitch in which we can truthfully say:

- We were the first firm to protect multinationals from cyber attack.
- We are the largest cybersecurity firm in North America.
- Gartner rates us as the most effective cybersecurity firm in the United States.

Want to be remembered? Find a category where you can be number one.

Shrink the Pond

Jackie Kruger runs marketing for the Minneapolis-based accounting and financial services consulting firm CliftonLarsonAllen. "I always tell my practice leads to 'shrink the pond.'" We love that phrase. Better to be a big fish in a small pond than a small fish in an endless ocean of near competitors.

When it comes to expert services, being undifferentiated is death. "Our company is the largest cloud-based HR software integrator for midsized accounting and law firms in the Southwest" is far better than, "We are a one-stop IT shop that helps clients design and build technology solutions."

It's old marketing advice, but timeless. Shrink the pond until you dominate your niche. Tom recently spoke with a top-25 accounting firm about business development.

> "Where are you looking to grow?"
> "We are focused on $500 million to $2 billion revenue companies."
> "What are some projects you have done recently where you did a really good job for the clients?"
> "We have worked with two mining companies to help them install state-of-the art enterprise risk-management systems."
> "That is a niche you could own. You could be the largest accounting firm focused on serving the mining industry."
> "We did a good job for those companies."
> "Try that as a focus for your business development—calling on mining company CFOs, sharing with them case studies on how you have helped similar firms. You have a right to dominate that niche which will be more effective than just saying you work with big companies."

The firm narrowed its focus, and their reputation for expertise in that niche grew. Soon, they were being invited to speak at mining industry panels, convening a best practices roundtable for mining CFOs that meets quarterly, hiring a retired mining executive as an advisor, and in general positioning themselves as the go-to accounting firm for global mining companies.

The rule is if you can't say you are the largest or best in a category, make your market definition smaller. *Shrink the pond.*

Good: We are the third-largest oil and gas lease consultant in North America.
Better: We are the largest oil and gas lease consultant in Texas.
Good: We specialize in business law.
Better: Voted the best franchise attorneys by the International Franchise Association for the last five years.

Specificity attracts. If you say you are the world's expert at Latin American food company audits, you will develop a name for yourself in that market. More importantly, when a Colombian mango juice manufacturer needs an audit, *they will remember you are in the business.*

The Bottom Line

Of course, being known as the largest oil and gas lease consultant in Texas or the best franchise attorney is good, but it is not enough. You also have to do good work. You have to back up your position in the marketplace with real expertise and then be able to own that statement of ability.

> You succeed by being good with people, but you also succeed by being an expert in something. Generalists do not succeed in the long run. Eventually you have to figure out where you're going to become deeply knowledgeable, and you have

to be able to show people that you have that knowledge. It's really hard for young people to figure what they want to specialize in early in their career, but the road to success, at least in our firm, comes from becoming a subject matter expert. You have to go deep.

—Ed Keller, Chief Marketing Officer, Navigant Consulting

How to Find Focus: The Power of Good Questions

Ask yourself:

- What project or product from the past twenty-four months are we most proud of?
- Which of our current clients would freak out if we disappeared tomorrow?
- Which work seems the most effortless for us?
- On which work do we rarely get pushback on price?
- What project or product is the most profitable?
- Which products or services would our core customers not miss if we stopped offering them tomorrow?
- In which markets do we not have any head-to-head competition?
- Who are our main competitors, and how are we different?

Hone Your Elevator Pitch

If niching and its power to drive *top-of-mind awareness* (TOMA) is a critical stepping stone on the client's path to engaging with you, the journey is completed with a clear and compelling articulation of what you do.

- A statement of your niche.
- A statement of whom you serve.
- A statement of how you help your clients.
- A statement of how you are different.

Let's bring this all together into an elevator pitch.

"Thompson is the largest family law practice in Georgia. We help families solve problems and figure out a better path forward using our staff of professionally trained mediators."

Thompson is the largest family law practice in Georgia. That's their niche. They help families. That is the statement of who they serve. They help figure out a better way forward. That is a statement of how the firm helps their clients. They use a staff of professionally trained mediators. That is how they are different.

And twice again, for practice.

"We're the nation's first and largest lead detection consultancy. We help public works professionals safeguard drinking water using the patented Potable Test System (PTS)."

"We're the oldest surf instruction shop in Maui. No one helps you catch a wave faster than the professionals at Rip Curl. Because old surfers know a bad day of surfing beats a good day at work."

But What If We Have Multiple Capabilities?

Dave Bayless provides expert services as part of his firm, Human Scale Business. An MBA, serial entrepreneur, former banker, and private equity investor, he brings a wealth of experience and knowledge to his clients. It's surprising, then, to hear him say that the biggest challenge he sees in his own practice and in the expert service practices of others is the tendency to be "intentionally vague."

We see this all the time with practice leads and consulting partners. We'll ask them, "What are the services you provide?" Their answer will be, "Depends on the problem."

Expert service providers do this for two reasons. First, they are smart and can legitimately offer help in a variety of different situations across industries and geographies. Second, they know new business is hard to find and if they get a nibble on the hook, their first instinct is to start reeling, regardless of whether the fish is in or out of season.

Dave reports he learned the need for focus the hard way, defining his consulting practice broadly, but over time narrowing it, and in so doing, expanding his right to own that niche.

There are two ways to grow a business. You can add new clients inside a tightly defined niche, or you can try to mine a dozen niches simultaneously. The temptation is always the latter even though your rate of growth is higher and your margins greater when you stick to where you have a right to "own" a space.

Early in my career, before I was a partner, I worked with captive insurance company structures, which is a niche area of tax, and a niche area in [the] insurance world. I wrote articles, wrote a book with another colleague, did the speaking circuit every time I could. I was at all the seminars where I would bump into all [the] experts. I became branded inside the firm as an expert and was able to work around [the] country on opportunities. To this day, people call me even though now I am a leader in the firm. I found that once an expert, always an expert. Sometimes when I talk with young people, they are hesitant to go deep into something. I say it is like being a surfer. You find a great wave and you are having a good time riding the wave. You're having great success but then the wave crashes to shore. That's okay. You proved you could ride the wave and ride it success[fully]. It had its normal end. Find more waves. Get back out there. If you think in our profession, there aren't going to be more waves, you are crazy. You niche yourself and then re-niche yourself over time.

—Greg Engel, KPMG, National Service Line Leader, Federal Tax Services

It is a mistake to think that niching yourself precludes shifting your niche over time. Once you have a niche, you don't have to live there forever. You can keep that home and then go find another. It is also a mistake to think that niching yourself precludes taking on work that exists outside of the niche. You can find your niche and expand your expertise at the same time. The important thing to know is that going to market with a "we-can-do-anything" approach is weak, while clearly articulating who you are and the professional conversation you want to have is powerful.

Tactics—What Works

The trick is to communicate what you do best to those you wish to serve. You can do that in the following ways:

- **Shake hands.** Wherever you go, one of your missions should be to make new friends. Meet people, shake their hands, ask them about themselves, and when they ask you what you do, be prepared with a statement that defines your niche and abilities in as few words as possible. "I run a consulting practice that helps plant managers reduce accident rates by using data to help them understand what gives rise to accidents. We are the largest such firm in California." You should say that at an industry conference but also during cocktail hour at your wife's law firm picnic.

- **Write.** You should write to get your name out there, and at the end of everything you put your name to you should include a tag: "Jamal Blanc is a managing director of Clearview, the oldest marketing services firm in the Southwest. There he runs a practice focused on website design and SEO for B2B companies."

- **Speak.** Same goes for speaking gigs. The reason to give a speech is so that you can include your biography in the program. That bio is not just a chance to stack up your jobs and degrees; it is a chance to tell people what you do. Give the speech and watch how people come up to you afterwards and share their interests and needs around that same topic.

- **Cold call.** If you read about someone in a trade magazine or see a link to a blog they have written, reach out and schedule time to learn more. When you chat, you'll have a chance to state who you are and what your interests are. Practice that moment. Be able to articulate exactly what you do and who you do it for.

- **Target your advertising.** Broad advertising has limited value in expert services. It is not that it doesn't have an effect; it is just that the return on investment is questionable. The exception to that rule is targeted ads that explain what you do. Tightly segmented ads in trade journals or at trade shows or conferences can be a great way of telling your story.

- **Tune up your website.** You probably already have a website, but does it communicate your niche clearly? Clients come to your site to better understand what you do. Make sure your website clearly articulates three things: what you do, who you serve, and how you're unique.

Clients buy because they have heard of you and they understand what you do, but there is more. They have to feel like what you do can help them. We call this interest.

11

Element 3: I Am Interested

These Are My Goals

The sun shone through the office window, filtering through the leaves in the Denver office park. We'd just given our pitch. The woman across the walnut conference table took careful notes and asked solid questions, all good signs in our mind. Maybe we'd finally sold something!

We offered up a trial balloon.

"Based on what you've said, it sounds like you would find it useful for us to scope out a project that includes the following three elements . . ."

She looked back at us, her voice catching ever so slightly, as she searched for the right words. Our eyes twitched imperceptibly. We had a nibble, maybe even a strike, but the fish was swimming away. We could feel it.

"I really like you guys. . . . However, we don't have a need for your services."

In the journey that each prospective client travels, Element 3—Interest—is often where there are bumps in the road. This is when clients begin making decisions about whether to invest further time with you.

You've done a great job of building awareness of your firm with a prospective client. The initial awareness could have come from a wide range of possible sources: a solid referral from a trusted source, someone you met at a conference, a lead from someone within your firm, an inbound email from your website or blog, or a cold call to someone you'd like to get to know. In any case, the prospective client is now aware of you. That's good. Without awareness of you or your firm, there's no getting to step two.

Now, imagine you've also done a good job of helping the new prospect clearly understand *who you are, what you do best, who you serve, and how you are unique*—the key ingredients of an effective marketing strategy. Good news. All of your messaging efforts have paid off; the new prospect knows exactly what you do and how you are different from potential competitors. This understanding may have come from your website, marketing collateral, a cold email, the first telephone call, or a face-to-face conversation. He or she may not understand in great detail all of your strengths at this point, but you've done a good job of initially positioning yourself in a way that is clearly understood and distinctive.

Now comes the moment of truth: Will the prospective client decide to spend more time with you or not? It is when you find whether you're making real progress in a new business relationship or things are about to stall. When the decision is positive, you have a follow-on call or meeting to further discuss opportunities, or maybe they even request a proposal. If not, you might hear, "It has been great to learn about your offering. While we are not at a point of doing anything like this, I appreciate your reaching out." But more often than not, the prospect simply stops returning your calls or taking your meetings. In the latter case, you're often left scratching your head, "What went wrong?"

Indeed, what *did* go wrong? Let's take a moment and unpack the client's mental calculus to better understand how and why they made the decisions they did.

In order for prospective clients to continue spending time with you, they have to conclude that:

- What you do is *relevant* to them and their goals. You have to solve a problem, support a strategic initiative, or promote an organizational agenda that is on their plate.
- Your services must promise to have a significant positive *impact* on those goals. They must "move the needle" on revenue growth, cost reduction, business performance, or another important metric.

Driving in the Right Direction

One of the simple things that is often overlooked when I've talked to some of the younger partners [about business development] is, "Have you asked your client for their business plan for the next one to three years?" Just asking the simple question, "Could you share with me your business plan, how your department's being evaluated, what your goals are over the next year, two, or three?" sets you apart from your competition. I have found over the years that clients often say, "Well, nobody's ever asked me that question. Of course, I'll share that with you." But I've never had anybody say, "Well, that's a confidential matter. I'm not going to share that with you." It's really more of, "Well, I'd love to walk you through how we're being evaluated and what our plans are and some thoughts around that."

—Chuck Walker, Partner, Global Leader
of Asset Management, Tax, KPMG

In order for a prospective client to be interested in spending much time in getting to know you, you have to be perceived as being relevant to them. Our work must have the potential to solve a perceived problem or advance an agenda for a prospective client. If it doesn't, our work isn't relevant.

Say, for example, you're a turnaround specialist—someone with deep experience in reviving troubled manufacturing companies with serious financial issues often involving bankruptcy. Your work is relevant to a relatively small number of companies at any given time.

You've just taken your seat in first class on American 2309, heading home from Chicago to Dallas on a Wednesday evening.

"It's been one of those days," your seatmate sighs. "I need a drink." You start to chat as he orders Jack on ice. You order a coffee because you've got to run some more numbers on the injection molding company you've been working with in a Chicago suburb that is going through Chapter 11.

As the conversation continues, you learn your seatmate is the owner of a company that makes industrial fasteners, and his bankers have just cut off his five-million-dollar line of credit. The company his father founded in 1962 won't have enough money to make payroll this month. He's on his way to visit another banker in Texas to see about some new financing. He knows things are getting dire. His ears perk up when he learns that you're a turnaround specialist who works with privately held manufacturing companies. By the time you get off the plane at

Dallas/Ft. Worth International Airport, you've scheduled a meeting in ten days to see about helping his company. Your expertise is highly relevant to your new friend who has suddenly found himself at risk of losing it all.

Harder, though, is when a prospective client doesn't even know they have a potential problem with which you can help. In IT services, for example, you may know more about the problems a prospective client faces than it does. You are selling a credence good after all. You diagnose and offer the cure. You offer a cyber-security solution, but if the company has never had a cyber attack or isn't aware their systems are particularly vulnerable, you face an uphill climb as you work to create interest in what you do. That is until the chief information officer gets a call at 4 a.m. telling him his company's customer credit card database just got hacked.

Harder still is that, for many of us, our offerings are discretionary. Our clients don't have to work with us; they elect to engage to work with us because it is consistent with their strategy. Harry Wallace, who started the firm Tom runs, is fond of saying, "If you're a doctor and someone falls down on a plane, you have an obligation to help." That's true but more common are clients who need our help but who don't know it. What's the doctor to do then?

Making a Meaningful Difference

You might recommend that your client move its call center from India to Nebraska to save the company two million dollars. This is a significant savings for a five-hundred-million company, but not necessarily to a fifty-billion-dollar company. Your work or expertise must make a meaningful difference on a prospective client's success because value is relative.

If your prospect is the head of business development for a Fortune 100 firm, the question to ask is does your work have the potential to bring in tens or hundreds of millions in new revenue? The difference is material. That doesn't mean your services aren't useful. It just means that they don't have the potential to have a meaningful impact on the progress of those goals on which the business development chief is measured.

Part of being material is to have a point of view. Saying what you see is a form of listening and establishing relevance. You observe a company and report back on what it looks like to you.

> The [goal] is to be a problem solver, creating solutions for clients. If you can tell them a solution before they recognize they have a problem they need, you're best positioned to win the business.
> —Jimmy Rose, Bank of America Merrill Lynch (retired)

In the end, a potential client is either interested in what you offer, or they are not. It fits with their priorities or it doesn't. This can be hard to hear, but always remember that a client can really want to work with you but just have more pressing objectives on their plate. Never mistake lack of interest with readiness. They are very different. Interest means you are focused on problems that make a difference in your buyer's life. Not being ready can be an issue of resources or politics. If someone is not interested in your service, you should leave them alone. If they are not ready, you should stay in touch.

If they are not interested, don't just walk away, though. Ask for a referral. "We'd love to work with your firm, but I understand what we do is not a fit for your priorities. Who do you think might be interested in something like this? Would you mind if I said you suggested I reach out to them?"

Second, concede but quickly recast. "We understand. You're busy redoing your website and can't think about developing a custom CRM platform right now. Maybe there is another way to think about this. Not us as a vendor to be managed, but more an outsourced partner that is making progress on a platform so that after the website is done, you have something to consider."

Tactics—What Works

Getting the second call or meeting is an important component in building a relationship. It signals that what you have to offer is of value. Here are concrete steps to up the odds of getting a second call.

Communicate clearly. Clearly articulate two key items: Why you are relevant to your customer's world, and how you can have a substantial impact on their agenda.

Research. Communicating clearly presupposes you know your customers' objectives. The truth, however, is that most of the time you don't have any clue what your client is focused on. You might speculate that they should be interested in raising revenues or cutting costs, but you don't know if that is their focus or if they are worried about a downsizing, getting a new boss, the feedback they got on the last project they managed, a speech the CEO just gave, or a host of other factors that drive how they define their objectives in any given quarter. Assuming a human being is driven by a single motivation is also silly. Every one of us is a stew of different motivations. Your job is to unpack those motivations as they are revealed to you. "Seeing-eye dogs" inside of organizations can help. If you know people in the industry or, better still, at the company you are trying to serve, they can give you color on the person you are trying to help. Interviewing for information in this way can help you learn the backstory on a company that, as much as anything you say or do, will determine interest. Reading what has been published is also helpful. One thing we like to do these days is to watch YouTube videos of interviews or speeches by the executives we are trying to serve. Nothing helps you get into your prospect's head better. Or watch a company's CEO speak. They are often very forthcoming about where they are trying to lead the company. Chances are they are telling your prospect the same thing. Finally, look at the case studies a firm puts on their website. This is the work of which they are most proud. You can be sure they want to do more of it.

Stop talking and listen. Remember when we said it's best to start from your customer's perspective, not from your own? To think about the buyer's journey, not the seller's journey? News flash, that's hard to do. It's like we are programmed to tout what we do, not listen to some middle manager prattle on about their issues. *Yet, listening is precisely what we need to do most.* When presenting, limit yourself to ten minutes. After that, ask questions. "When I spoke just now, I suggested you might be interested in how we have helped other companies lift their procurement process into the cloud, but I was guessing there. How is it that you see your procurement operation?" Asking questions starts a conversation that helps both parties work toward an eventual goal. You start by suggesting something that might be helpful. Your client quickly comes back and says you're off substantially. "We've been doing cloud-based procurement for two years now. What worries me now is security." That response gives you an opportunity to ask more questions. "Are you mainly worried about cloud security, or is it the lack of security on your end that is the problem?" Again, you proffer a thesis and then give them a chance to come back to you. "On our end, mostly. I have to collect data from five business units spread across sixteen countries, and I worry we're not completely protected. I told myself this year I'd audit the network and take measures to make sure we don't drop the ball." Now you're getting somewhere.

Add value first. Just as we are tempted to talk to our clients about how we can help them and not listen to how they want to be helped, it's also true that in our rush to demonstrate our prowess, we fail to add value and instead we just advertise our skill. The problem with that approach is that people don't like being sold to. They don't mind having a conversation with people they don't know, but they have to feel like they are getting something in the exchange. A partner in a Big Four accounting firm described how she thinks about meeting with would-be clients: "I tell them one thing they don't know about their competitors, one thing they don't know about their own company and one thing they don't know about us. I don't want to just ask for information when I visit them. I want to bring them information."

If you're a private equity firm or a venture capital firm, you may have various assets in your portfolio that are relevant to us in the healthcare capital markets group. We find ways to sit down and have meetings, or phone calls, or just send emails with content that's relevant to them. This serves as a way to deepen a conversation on a given company—really, anything we can do to continue a dialogue, whether it's something that's a near-term action item or not, helps build that relationship. [The goal] is to be the person they call when they're ready to actually do something.
                                        —Jack Bannister, Goldman Sachs

In the world of consulting and professional services sales, "Always Be Closing" is out. Now it's "Always Be Listening."

Asking Questions

The ability to conduct a strong interview is, perhaps, the most important arrow in a consultant's quiver. Shot with confidence, it pierces the awkwardness that naturally exists between two professionals who do not know each other.

Tom's daughter is twenty-two and just graduated from college. He helped her move from Atlanta to Washington, DC, settling her in before she started her first job. U-haul trailer in tow, they had plenty of time during the ten-hour drive to talk in the car. Somewhere around Greenville, South Carolina, she asked him about networking. She said her mentors told her to cultivate a network in her new job, that it would be key to her success in DC, but added, "Sometimes it feels awkward to chat at a cocktail party with people you don't know about more professional topics that aren't 'social.'"

"Ask questions," Tom said. "Everyone likes to be asked questions."

His daughter looked puzzled.

"Ask them about their job. Get them to open up. 'What do you do? Oh, the EPA? What role do you play there? What are the three biggest challenges facing the agency right now? What are the competing schools of thought on how to best respond? What are other countries doing? Is there something to be learned from their experience?'"

"It sounds like you are interrogating them."

"I'm telling you—a funny thing happens when you ask questions about people. They think you're smart—and they enjoy the conversation."

You might think people like being interviewed because they like to hear themselves talk—that it's vanity, a shiny mirror we put in front of people that lets them admire themselves – but we disagree. We think thoughtful questions are an invitation to create new understanding.

Asking great questions gives those with whom you are speaking the valuable gift of insight, perhaps verbalized for the first time. You are saying to them, "You work all day in a specific world. That gives you a unique and informed perspective that is valuable. What is it? Share with me your wisdom."

When a prospective client is *aware of you*, understands exactly *what you do*, and is *interested in the services* that you provide, things really begin to get interesting. This is when an important mental transition occurs; prospective clients begin to ask themselves not just what you do and if they need you, but *"is this person really good at what they do and will they deliver on their promises?"*

12

Element 4: I Respect Your Work

You Have the Right Stuff to Help Me

Now things are starting to heat up.

1. The client knows who you are.

2. They understand what you do.

3. They are interested because what you do is relevant to their priorities.

All that is well and good, but they are far from choosing to work with you. Before they can comfortably engage, they have to take your measure. The pros we interviewed all agreed: nearly every one of them spoke of the need for potential clients to trust you.

Our view is that trust is a big word that sits like an umbrella over two equally important concepts that are usefully separated. The first is "trust" as a near-synonym for the word "credible." A client has to feel there is a high likelihood you will be able to do what you say you will do. The second is "trust" as a near-synonym for "loyal." A client has to feel you have their best interests at heart.

- I trust you will get the job done.
- I trust you have my back.

To avoid confusion, we call the first of these two "trusts" *respect*. When a client respects your experience, background, and track record, they are confident you will get the job done.

Billy Newsome, a good friend of Doug's, is partner with Nexsen Pruet, a leading Southeastern law firm headquartered in Columbia, South Carolina. Listen to him talk about the importance of establishing personal credibility:

> Much of what you have to learn about the practice of law is through experience, interacting with clients and learning what their decision points are, and how to listen to their concerns. And you need a certain amount of experience to be able to talk about those issues. You don't necessarily have to be able to sit down in the initial meeting and provide them the solution to their problem, because often it's not that simple. But you do have to have a certain basic level of expertise that comes through when you're talking to the client. If you can't demonstrate that, they probably aren't going to have the confidence to hire you. And so, I think that

getting your ten thousand hours of experience and becoming an expert in your field of practice, is necessary to be able to then go out and sell your services.

We will discuss the second trust, the one that has to do with whether a client believes you will do the right thing and choose their interests over your own, in the next chapter. For now, let's focus on what causes a potential client to respect what you bring to the table—what Billy is calling his ten thousand hours of expertise. Think of this chapter, which is focused on respect, as the way in which a client uses their head to evaluate you. It is a left-brain calculation on whether or not the respect they have for your background gives them enough confidence to rely on you with a project of high consequence to their lives. It's when a client tallies up the pros and cons of engaging with you.

Track Record

For more than a year, Tom was on the road raising money for an inaugural private equity fund. He and his partner, Phil Collins, called on all manner of affluent individuals and family offices, jetting from New York to San Francisco and from Dallas to Chicago.

"It's great to meet you," Phil would say. "Maybe it makes sense for us to give you a little background on us and then walk you through our investment thesis."

Tom would give a ten-sentence summary of his experience, and then Phil would give his. Tom emphasized his background with operating companies. Phil would follow making the case that he was the investor, that he had apprenticed with a respected self-made billionaire, gone to Harvard Business School, worked at McKinsey, and then became the youngest partner in a large, established private equity firm.

In giving these short bios, they were setting out their credentials—establishing who they were in the very specific sense of establishing their right to be in the room.

Are You Legit?

The history of modern diplomacy starts in the thirteenth century when the commander of Milan's private army, Francesco Sforza, grabbed the reins of power and named himself the Duke of Milan. He quickly established relations across what would become northern Italy; opening permanent embassies in each of the city-states and sending out ambassadors with letters authorizing them to speak on behalf of Milan. Soon all of the European states were establishing missions in other countries, and the modern diplomatic corps and the conventions we know today were born, including the ritual of presenting and accepting of ambassadorial credentials.

That was Phil and Tom, submitting their *bona fides* in front of potential investors. "Here's our background. We're the kind of partnership in which you might imagine investing. We belong here."

After presenting their credentials, Tom and Phil would pivot to their thesis, giving examples of the companies in which they planned to invest. There would be questions and answers, and then came the only question that mattered.

"Tell me about your investment track record."

"Track record" is everything in investing, and it is that way with potential consulting and professional service clients as well: potential clients want to hear about your track record or what you have done successfully for others.

"Tell me about your experience doing digital transformations for other companies."

"Have you ever worked with a company of our size?"
"Will you be working on the project or will it be a more junior person?"
"What kind of return on investment can we expect?"
"Do you have case studies?"
"May I speak with references?"

All of these questions are focused on gauging the likelihood that you can do what you say you can do. That's because in a consulting or professional services sale, the past is prologue. What you have done for past clients is the only fact-based way to evaluate you as a partner. Everything else is words—assertions and promises without evidence.

Adam Waytz, working at Northwestern's Kellogg School of Business's Trust Project, studies trust from the perspective of psychology, neuroscience, and psycho-physiology. Waytz offers this definition of trust: "Does this person behave in a way I can consistently predict?"

Paul Bloom shares this perspective in *Effective Marketing for Professional Services*, his seminal 1984 article in *Harvard Business Review*:

Because buyers of professional services are often uncertain about the criteria to use in selecting a professional, they tend to focus on one question: Have you done it before? People prefer to use accountants and management consultants who have worked in their industry previously, lawyers who have litigated cases just like theirs, architects who have designed buildings like the one they want to build, and surgeons who have performed the needed surgical procedure hundreds of times. Using an experienced professional makes a risky purchase seem less risky. Among other things, if anything goes wrong, a buyer may avoid being blamed by superiors or family members for carelessly choosing an unproven professional.

Establishing Credibility

Part of a client's reaction might be in response to the size of your firm. If you're a five hundred-person firm with offices in ten cities in the United States and you're talking to ExxonMobil about implementing a global ERP system that will require two hundred and fifty people in a dozen countries, the client might reasonably conclude you're not big enough to do the job. As good as your pitch is, ExxonMobil is likely to hire an Accenture or IBM.

As with most things in life, there's a pecking order among consulting and professional services firms. Some are more prestigious than others. McKinsey, Bain, and BCG are perceived by many to be in the top tier of strategy consulting firms. If you work for one of these three, your firm's reputation will have a halo effect on your own reputation. Conversely, if you are a partner in a twenty-person boutique strategy shop, you may have to work a bit harder to prove your credibility.

It is not that working with a small firm doesn't have its advantages. Not every company can afford to hire a large firm. Additionally, not every client wants to hire a large firm. Some prefer working with smaller firms because they believe they'll get more attention and better service. The point is that, despite this, your firm's relative prestige is the coat you wear as you brave the storms of the marketplace.

Your personal credentials are also important. It may mean "Do you have the proper degrees or certifications?" in professions like law, accounting, engineering, and architecture. But certifications aren't always professional gates; they can also be accessories that signal your knowledge of a field and commitment to it. For example, Certified Financial Analyst (CFA) or Certified Financial Planner (CFP) in the financial services industry communicates competence.

For some people, the caliber of school makes a difference. Each professional services field has its own pecking order of educational status. Did you go to a top-tier school like Yale Law, Harvard Business School, or Stanford's School of Engineering? If so, you're assumed to be capable. If you didn't go to one of the elite schools, it doesn't mean you're not smart, it just means that you don't benefit from the school's reputation. It means you have a little further to walk to show clients your intelligence and ability.

To some, credibility may be "Do you look and act the part?" For every profession, there's a way professionals dress and carry themselves. For investment banking, it may be a bespoke suit or Jimmy Choo shoes. In advertising and tech, jeans and more casual footwear are the norm. How you look helps form would-be clients' first impressions and works to build up or tear down your credibility.

When Doug was at business school on the East Coast, it was the investment banks, management consulting firms, and Fortune 100 companies that recruited graduates most heavily. Students were expected to arrive at interviews wearing their very best suits. You were quickly sized up by these companies based upon whether you "looked the part." If you arrived inappropriately dressed, you probably didn't get a call back for a second interview.

One of the companies recruiting during his second year was a large West Coast software company. It was the cool company at the time, and students were drooling over the chance to work for the company. Every student wore their nicest suit to this tech company's interview except for one. Paul had lived on the West Coast before graduate school and knew a bit more about the tech industry's culture. Instead of wearing a Brooks Brothers suit to the interview, he wore jeans and a polo shirt. Paul got the only job offer. Was it because of the jeans? Maybe not. Was it because he understood the tech industry's culture? Maybe. Was it because he stood out from the other students and signaled that he was original? Perhaps. Was he the best candidate from the school? Hard to say. The point of the story is that what you wear and how you act matter in establishing your initial credibility.

Can a Client Rely on You to Get the Job Done?

Clients ask themselves a simple question: Do they think you and your team can do the job? The answer is binary. If yes, proceed. If no, do not pass "Go."

Potential clients might know a firm (they are aware of you), know you are active in a specific vertical (they understand what you do), and have a problem they are eager to solve (they are interested), but at some point, they need to be assured that you can do the work. They look at you and, using their head, they weigh the benefits versus the costs of engaging your firm. The scales tip in your direction when a prospective client:

- Believes you can add significant value to their projects
- Believes that the economic, strategic, political, and emotional benefits of what you do outweigh the financial, career, emotional, and time investments and risks
- Believes you can actually do what you say you can do
- Believes that your team is the best option among other choices

The scales tip when they look at the sum of who you are and what you have done and conclude that there is a high likelihood you will be able to deliver value to their firms *just like you have always done*.

Tactics—What Works

Here's how clients evaluate your track record and what that means for you.

- **Are You Relevant?** Prospective clients clients ask themselves: *Have you done this sort of work before for other clients who are of similar size, operate in the same geography, and/or play in a certain industry?* There is a temptation when speaking with would-be clients to use the same story or case study. You get good at telling it, and others have found it compelling. But it's lazy. Better to tailor your story or case study to the potential client with whom you are hoping to work. Yes, they want to hear about your high-profile prestige engagement, but they are more interested in learning about work you have done for firms who are in their *nearly exact* situation.

  Say you own a coffee shop chain with one hundred and twenty-six locations in six states. You are interested in doing a merchandising reset and are interviewing merchandising consultants. Everyone shows up with examples of their work. One firm did a reset for a hardware chain in the Southeast, a fast-casual restaurant design in the UK, and a merchandising plan for a 13,000-unit international convenience store chain. The second firm spun out of the Starbucks internal merchandising team and has done merchandising sets for more than twenty coffee shop chains as well as a dozen juice and smoothie operations. Who do you think is more compelling to the client? The relevant experience of the ex-Starbucks team probably wins the day. Remember how niching helps prospective clients remember you? Your concentrated experience also helps win the deal.

- **Are You Reputable?** Potential clients don't just ask if you have done the work before, but have you done a good job? What do others say about you?

    Old timers like to say that "delivery sells," where the quality of your work is the table on which your reputation sits.

All of my work has come from referrals and repeat business. That's it. So, doing good work is the key because if you do good work, you'll get repeat business and referrals. I think it's both pretty simple and pretty complex at the same time. When you get an opportunity, do a darn good job with it, don't burn any bridges, and be very pleasant when you are referred to someone and have a conversation. Always try and be helpful even if you don't take an assignment.

—Graham Anthony, founder/principal, Anthony Advisors

Good work is the ether through which word-of-mouth travels. You do good work for a client, and then when one of their friends likes what they see or expresses a need, your client says, "I should put you in touch with the firm I used. I'd highly recommend them."

Over and over you hear about the need to be clear about impact. What difference did you make for clients? Hard figures always outweigh soft contribution statements. Think of the investors judging Phil and Tom. How much money have you made for people in the past? Track record is the best predictor of future results.

Following Up: How to Write
a Compelling Deck

Carlie Breen has been on five hundred introductory calls. She has a uniquely engaging way of speaking with those she does not know that makes her a natural at making new friends. One thing she has noticed is that as the thirty-minute introductory call comes to a close, there is always a pregnant pause when the prospective client knows that they should talk about next steps. Rarely does a prospective client say, "Sounds good. How do we get started?" Much more likely, they push you off. "They seek to create space to consider what you have said to them," says Carlie. Enter "The Deck."

"Do you have a short piece that describes what you do and perhaps what you have done for others?" This is the most common end to an introductory conversation with someone you think you might be able to help with your expert services. They ask you for what is essentially a brochure of your services.

"They want to talk to others on their team," says Carlie. "But they also want to test you. How quickly do you turn something around? Is it high quality? We try and send out a deck by at least the next business day."

A strong deck includes the following four elements:

- **A statement of capabilities.** Can you clearly explain what you do in a way your grandmother would understand yet focused enough that you are positioned as one of the foremost leaders in your niche? Your audience here is not the person you spoke with on the phone; it is the colleague or boss to whom the deck is forwarded. You need to be able to explain your value proposition to them using a handful of printed words.

- **Case studies.** This is where you draw from your library of experiences to describe how you have helped others in similar situations. Make sure the examples are relevant. A small firm is going to wonder if the success you delivered on behalf of three Fortune 500 firms can be duplicated for them if they are much less well known or command far fewer resources. Likewise, if all of your cases involve small clients, a large firm is going to wonder if you have the chops to play in the big game. Carlie suggests that a good case study includes the task you were assigned by a client, what you did, and finally, the resultant return on investment for the client.

- **A credibility page.** It is said that, "No one was ever fired for hiring IBM." Clients have problems that need to be solved, but when engaging with you, they want air cover. They don't want to be defending their decision to hire a firm with no track record and no references to tackle an important challenge. That could be a quick way to lose their job. The credibility page in the deck is where you include logos of important present and past clients. Who you have worked with in the past helps build your credibility—the idea that you can be trusted with a task and that you will do what you say.

- **Contact information.** This may seem silly. You attached the deck in an email that has your contact information, but once sent, decks take on a life of their own. They get forwarded on to others you have never met. Make sure you leave your calling card.

Do You Have the Right Team?

Clients ask themselves: *Who are the people with whom we will be working?* Once Tom was given advice by a project manager at Accenture to include his bio and the bio of his team in a project proposal. "People want to know who they are working with. If you don't include impressive bios, they will assume the worst and that they are going to get some yahoo you hired off the street."

Bios always include the same elements:

- **What is your education?** When selling credence goods where the client has to trust in an unknown outcome, education is often a proxy for capability. One of the smartest people Tom ever worked with was the county manager of a large suburban county in northern Virginia who didn't have a college degree. That's fine, but it was harder to sell. In general, the more the better—degrees, advanced degrees, published papers, executive courses, adjunct professor positions, graduate school advisory councils—all these things send the signal that you are both capable and current. But what if you don't have a pedigree like a dog at the Westminster Kennel Club? Speak to your experience. Tom's friend won the big job in Fairfax County because he had done yeoman's work for the county since he started out as a map-maker at eighteen. Cyber-security experts often do not have any degrees at all, but they can keep you up all night telling you about the bugs they found and the fixes they wrought on behalf of consequential clients.

- **What is your title?** Clients peruse websites and LinkedIn to understand the level of the person with whom they are going to work. Is it a senior, experienced person or a junior person? This may be unfair to the newbie and overly generous to the long-time professional, but clients tell us that seniority matters because it stands in for credibility absent any other measure.

- **What is your specialty?** By describing a niche, a professional is asserting her or his domain expertise.

Paula Everhardt is a Senior Director with Avatar, having joined the firm from Hewlett Packard in 1999 where she served as vice president of revenue assurance. She has worked for fifteen of the twenty-five largest financial services companies on projects that drove down loss rates from between 21 percent and 36 percent. She teaches data analytics at Columbia Business School and has written a number of articles on how big data can drive higher collection rates for the *Journal of Finance Accounting*. She has been featured on the pages of *Forbes*, *Bloomberg*, and the *Wall Street Journal* on the subject of cloud-based revenue assurance and speaks regularly before conferences of revenue assurance professionals and is the past president of the Global Revenue Assurance Professional Association. Ms. Everhardt graduated *summa cum laude* from the University of Michigan Ross School of Business and has an undergraduate degree in accounting from Eastern Michigan University.

If you heard that Paula was going to design and execute a revenue assurance initiative for the regional bank system you run, what would your reaction be? You'd be thrilled.

How Much Experience Do You Have?

Clients ask: *How long have you been doing this work?* Is it your longstanding core competency, or are you just saying, "Sure, we can do that."? List assignments you have worked on even if they were when you were part of another firm. Clients extrapolate what you have done to what you will likely do for them. The more data points the better.

Do You Have Real Expertise?

Clients ask: *Do you know what you are talking about?* Ford Harding, author and business development consultant, puts it this way in his excellent book, *Rain Making*:

> When I hire a professional, I want an expert. Publications provide one proof of who is real and who isn't. Published work tells me that the author must have substantial experience and that she has reflected more deeply on her business than some. All other things being equal, the article will weigh more heavily than someone's self-acclamation.

> Says, Don Scales, CEO of Investis, a leading digital media company: "You have to have substance or all the style in the world won't do any good."

There are two ways to judge expertise. The first is to be an expert yourself and take a colleague's measure. If you do faculty recruitment for medical colleges and meet someone else in that line of work and they can't name four medical colleges, you know they're full of it. If, on the other hand, they do recruiting for Johns Hopkins and Baylor, you are likely to be impressed and talking shop in short order.

Below is a bio torn from the headlines. As we are writing, President Trump just named a new lawyer to run defense for him. Meet Ty Cobb as described on his firm's website:

> Bet-the-company litigation calls for a unique combination of skills, experience, and track record. Ty Cobb, a long-time leader at Hogan Lovells, has been widely recognized as one

of the premier white collar, Securities and Exchange Commission (SEC) enforcement, and congressional investigations lawyers in the world. Clients managing crises, allegations of corruption, and other critical matters turn to Ty to guide them. In 2015, *Super Lawyers* magazine, in the featured article "The Kansas Peach," observed that Ty is "the big gun on whom powerful people rely." "Ty Cobb gets results the old-fashioned way," says Robert Weber, former general counsel for IBM. "He gets his fingernails dirty doing the hard work, he is relentless and he deeply cares about his client."

We really like the "bet-the-company" language. Who would you trust with your hardest problems? Someone who has been solving your kind of problems for many years. *That's because previous performance is the best predictor of future performance.*

The second way we judge expertise is by relying on proxy votes of confidence. Note how Ty Cobb's marketing person relies heavily on third parties to vouch for Ty's expertise. We are left with the feeling that if *Super Lawyers* and the former general counsel of IBM think Ty is a good guy, then he must be someone on whom we can rely.

What does your bio look like?

CHAPTER 13

Element 5: I Trust You

You Have My Best Interests at Heart

War raged in the Middle East as Operation Iraqi Freedom worked to root out Saddam Hussein and his Ba'athist regime in April 2003. General Tommy Franks initiated the invasion by sending sortie after sortie of planes to rain munitions down on the Presidential Palace. Then, shortly after dawn the day after the invasion, he commanded coalition troops to pour into the Basra Province from jumping off points near the Kuwait border. At the same time, a sea landing of Royal Marines, U.S. Marines, Polish commandos, and Seal Teams 4, 6, and 8 secured Iraq's only deep-water port as well as its oil and gas assets. This was followed by waves of additional air strikes against Hussein's command and control apparatus. The operation was a success, with Baghdad falling on April 9.

Both U.S. and Iraqi troops fought under very difficult circumstances that included the constant threat of chemical weapons. Yet, while the U.S. soldiers pushed forward relentlessly, the Iraqi soldiers retreated and surrendered in great numbers. As the fighting began, Dr. Lenny Wong, a retired lieutenant colonel working at the Army's War College in Carlisle, Pennsylvania, saw an opportunity. Military leaders are interested in knowing why soldiers fight. Because the combat was fresh and there were so many prisoners of war, he decided to quickly interview both U.S. and Iraqi troops and compare their motivations. Had they fought out of patriotism, in pursuit of justice, for money, out of revenge, or because they were being forced to? Did a difference in motivation account for differing behavior?

His research team flew to Iraq and traveled first to Camp Bucca in Umm Qsar, where they spoke with captured Iraqi soldiers. Then they went to Baghdad and Al Hillah where they interviewed members of the 3rd Infantry Division, the 101st Airborne Division, and the 1st Marine Division.

Their results were striking, "For Iraqi regular army soldiers, it was coercion," Dr. Wong writes. They fought because they were scared of what would happen to them if they did not.

But for U.S. soldiers, Dr. Wong and his team saw something different. "The most frequent response given for combat motivation was 'fighting for my buddies.' Soldiers answered with comments such as, 'Me and my loader were talking about it, and in combat the only thing that you really worry about is you and your crew.'"

These findings are consistent with similar studies done during the Vietnam War, World War II, and even the Civil War. Human beings will storm a fortified hill or charge out of a foxhole, bayonets fixed, less for a larger cause and more out of loyalty to their friends. Their friends are ultimately the people who cause them to fight with ferocity, even to the point of making the ultimate sacrifice.

This begs the question: Why do troops fight more for their buddies than they do for God, country, or money?

Dr. Wong's team surmised two reasons. "First, because of the close ties to other soldiers, it places a burden of responsibility on each soldier to achieve group success and protect the unit from harm. Soldiers feel that although their individual contribution to the group may be small, it is still a critical part of unit success and therefore important. As one soldier put it, 'I am the lowest-ranking private on the Bradley [fighting vehicle] . . . I did not want to let anyone down.' One Bradley commander (BC) spoke of the infantrymen in the back of his vehicle and the responsibility he felt for them: 'You have two guys in the back who are not seeing what is going on, and they are putting all their trust into the gunner and the BC. Whatever objects or obstacles or tanks or vehicles are in front of you, you are taking them out, because they don't know what is going on. They are just like in a darkroom. They can't do nothing. Having that trust . . . I guess that is one thing that kept me going.'"

The second reason men fought so hard for each other was that watching each other's back was a form of self-preservation. Said one U.S. soldier, "If you are going to war, you want to be able to trust the person who is beside you. If you are his friend, you know he is not going to let you down. . . . He is going to do his best to make sure that you don't die."

Trust

The notion of trust in others is ancient. It allows one buddy to lean on another. It is the sinew that binds communities together, enabling them to do together what they cannot do as individuals. It makes the group more powerful and protects individuals from outside threats.

Kent Grayson, a professor of marketing at Northwestern University's Kellogg School of Management, studies trust. For him, trust between people in a commercial setting involves three elements:

- Competence
- Honesty
- Benevolence

This closely tracks with what we said in the last chapter, namely that when we speak about trust, we often are saying either:

- I trust you will get the job done (what Grayson is calling competence).
- I trust you have my back on this, where "have my back" means a potential client thinks you are honest and looking out for their interests (in Grayson's terms, honestly and benevolence).

One is a "head" judgment. We talked about this in the previous chapter and called it respect for your work—the belief that after reviewing the evidence, such as your credentials, your track record, and your references—you are likely to get the job done. This kind of trust is an intellectual weighing of the evidence out of which a buyer makes an informed judgment, predicting a partner's future behavior.

"I think it always comes down to trust," says Graham Anthony, the principal and founder of Anthony Advisors. "Does [a consultant] have the ability to do a good job? Clients are trusting that if they come to you with their problem, you will help them solve it."

The second half of trust is a "heart" judgment. Here you are not asking if a practice lead can get the job done, but if they will put your interests first. Graham says, "Do you trust the person wishes you well?"

The consulting firm Bain describes this second form of trust this way: "Everything we do is guided by our True North—our unswerving commitment always to do the right thing by our clients, our people, and our communities."

When clients hear and feel this in their consulting and professional services partners, they are reassured that the firm they are hiring will act in the clients' interests. They believe their consultants are true agents for their interests and therefore trusted extensions of their reach and impact.

> It is axiomatic in the consulting profession that the consultant is the least important person in the room. It is the clients' interests that matter. The consultant must always act in the best interests of the client and must never do anything that could harm or damage the client. . . . Consultants are in a privileged position: they have access to a great deal of inside information about the client and they also have a position over the client company and its key decision makers. . . .
> They owe it to the client to ensure that a) they do no harm and b) they serve the client's interests at all times.
> —Morgen Witzel, *Management Consultancy*

Professor Grayson from Northwestern says trust is broken in cases of information asymmetry when either the buyer or the seller takes advantage of that asymmetry. The CEO of a biotech firm wants to figure out the best way to include a broad swath of middle managers in the long-term value they are helping to create. She hires an expert in compensation who has particularly strong experience in setting up stock option programs. Our client is at an information disadvantage. She is hiring a consultant because she doesn't really know the ins and outs of stock options. Trust would be broken if the consultant recommended a long, involved study of what options entail in order to increase the ticket price of the engagement, knowing that for the company in question there are really only two choices.

Trust Is the Whole Ball of Wax

Clients need to trust that we will do the right thing by them for three reasons:

1. *The leap of faith is large.* You are expert at computer security, but your clients are not. That is why they are asking for your help. If they had spent a lifetime studying cyber security and had seen every kind of hack imaginable, they wouldn't need you. But they aren't experts, and that's why they are considering engaging with you. That, though, requires a leap of faith. In fact, if you think about it, the less they know, the bigger the leap. The bigger the leap, the more they feel a kind of I-could-lose-my-job fear that makes them gnash their teeth and sleep poorly at night. That fear can be partly lessened by lots of confirming data—the kind of data that leads to respect—but they also need a sturdy bridge built out of trust before they can fully commit.

2. *It gets everyone past conflicts of interest.* Closely related to the need to trust your abilities is the need for a client to trust you've steered clear of conflicts of interest. A true professional would never recommend a software solution for a company on whose board of directors they sat without disclosing it. That would be a conflict. Nor would an attorney represent two parties in conflict with each other. Whose side would the attorney be on? One of the key pieces of

knowing that someone has our back is the bedrock confidence we have that our consultant isn't secretly "working for the other side."

3. *It drives better performance.* Clients know, even if subconsciously, that teams bound by trust are more effective. To worry about intentions acts like sludge in the drivetrain of commerce. "Trust is the lubrication that makes it possible for organizations to work," wrote Warren Bennis and Burton Nanus in *Leaders: Strategies for Taking Charge.* "An organization without trust is more than an anomaly, it's a misnomer, a dim creature of Kafka's imagination."

Tactics—What Works

Here are seven proven trust-builders to keep in mind as you build your network:

Time

Time is your ally when building trust. All things being equal, we trust people we have known for a long time more than people we just met. Repeated exposure to an expert builds familiarity, which builds trust.

One of the rainmakers that we interviewed for this book was Don Scales. Don was Doug's boss at A.T. Kearney where Doug got his start right out of B-school. Scales, currently the CEO of Investis, has had a more than thirty year career in management consulting. To Don, trust is an essential asset that takes a long time to earn. He offered this advice to those getting started:

Trust is built up one successful transaction at a time. If you're selling for the first time to a new client, then trust is going to be your biggest challenge. You have to make sure that you're transparent, you're communicating all the time, and that the client can see what's going on. If you have a good transaction the first time, then it's a little bit easier the second time, and then a lot easier the third time, etc. It's all built one good transaction at a time.

Just like a central element of *respect* is the ability to predict how someone is going to perform on the job, the ability to predict whether or not someone has your back drives *trust*. Humans are pattern recognition animals, and the longer someone has had your back, the more clients are likely to extrapolate that pattern and trust you going forward. This is why pros in the consulting and professional services business tell us that the simplest business development advice is to do quality work because once in the door, trust acts as a barrier to entry for your competition.

Of course, trust takes patience.

I cut my teeth in Australia and Asia back in the day when Asia wasn't really on the map for anybody here. I always advise Americans not to be too quick to try to get to the end. Americans are like the culture of just, "Let's get down to business," versus being willing to spend the time and effort to get to know people. I think Americans need to take a deep breath and just spend some time building relationships.

—Peter Bryant, managing director, Clareo

Friends of Friends

New business for consulting and professional services firms comes from three places—repeat projects with existing customers, people who recommend you, and new clients with whom you have no relationship at all.

Harry Wallace is fond of saying, "If you had to generate business in the next thirty days, you would always start with your current or past clients." Trust is a gate a new service provider must hurdle. If time is short, you would call the people who have worked with you and who already trust you, saving yourself what might be the most difficult step. Likewise, most practice leads understand that if they don't know someone working at a potential client, it's tough to get a foothold.

Somewhere in between is the world of referrals, where a client mentions an able vendor to a friend over cocktails. Some consulting and professional service providers have built robust practices by simply never leaving a conversation with a client before asking, "I am trying to expand my practice. If you feel we have done good work for you, with whom should I be speaking? Would you mind if I used your name reaching out to them?" Says Jeff Denneen, a partner at Bain, "It is all about referrals for us. We are the firm that invented the net promoter score after all." The net promoter score is a measure based on asking customers, "How likely is it that you would recommend our company/product/service to a friend or colleague?" It is primarily used as a proxy for quality—customers who give vendors high promoter scores are satisfied with what they have received—but it also highlights the fact that embedded in quality delivery is the potential to mine referrals.

Easier still is staying in touch when someone you have worked with as a client leaves their company. Help them with their job search if appropriate. It builds trust. What says "you have their back even when it is not in your immediate self-interest" more than helping someone find their next gig?

Working Shoulder-to-Shoulder

The benefits of consulting and professional services are not easily described. They are better demonstrated. Smart practice leads look for opportunities to work alongside people, knowing that it is a chance to show competence and that character is revealed in those long hours in the windowless conference room or chatting back and forth late at night.

Doing the Right Thing

This seems obvious, that you should always do the right thing for your client, but in the real world "the right thing" can often come in varying shades of gray. Making the call on what is *right* and what is *wrong* lives at the margin. This is why it's important to land on the side of protecting your client whenever the call is close.

> Clients have to trust you. They have to trust that you will do the work, you'll put in the work, and that you'll do what you say you're going to do. They've got to trust that you've got honesty and integrity on your side . . . so that what you deliver is truthfully what you said you would deliver and the best that the market can provide.
> —Sarah Arnot, formerly of Accenture and Spencer Stuart

Remember, clients are watching you, taking your measure, one small decision at a time. Trust is the accumulation of those impressions.

- Did you report bad news quickly?
- Did you call in reinforcements on your dime when the unexpected arrived?
- Did you cut short your vacation to accommodate a presentation that was important to your program manager?

- Did you stay someplace reasonable and not dine at the most over-the-top restaurant in town?
- Did you absorb the unexpected expense of turning your crew around mid-flight to correct a problem?
- Were you mindful of your stakeholder's need to manage their internal politics?
- Were you discreet, keeping all confidences?
- Did you put your client's needs first?

Like a poker player studying how you respond to cards, clients read how you will likely act in the future. In each case, how you answer the questions above is a character tell.

A senior McKinsey partner shared this story with us:

> We were approached by the client about a particular topic. But as we did the early thinking about what was our unique value proposition, we realized two things really quickly. One, it wasn't actually going to be worth their time or money to do this with us, and that there was actually a better business partner who happened to be a competitor of ours. We went back to them and said, "We don't think we're the right people to serve you on this, but here are the three things that we do think you should be thinking about and we'd be happy to work on the third [piece]." The client was taken aback because they were ready to sign on the dotted line. This was not a competitive proposal, they were, like, "We want you to do this. Come on in and start this." But the partner actively turned it down. It's what we call at McKinsey a "values moment," and I was super-inspired by this. And then over the period of time, we earned a sort of a trusted adviser status with them. They trusted us because we didn't force our services when it would have been easy to just make the money.

Tell the Truth

It is easy to tell the truth when it means more business for you, but sometimes the truth means telling a client something that is not in your best interest. This is when our commitment to the long-term interests of our clients shines through even brighter, because our clients know it would be easier for us to avoid sharing what we see. Nothing builds trust faster.

Screwing Up

Screwing up on an engagement is never good. It involves *mea culpas*, embarrassment, lost time, hours that cannot be billed, and hard conversations with your team over stiff drinks. But it comes with a silver lining. It's a chance to promptly and without equivocation accept full and complete responsibility. It's also a chance to make good on what is bad.

Tom used to be the chief operating officer of a bread store franchise, Great Harvest Bread Co. He remembers how owners of those stores would call people who returned poorly baked bread "breadboard angels." Store owners would tell him that when someone returns bread, it is a chance to tell them, "Thank you for caring enough about this store and our product to let us know," and it gave them a chance to give the customer a "Ten Loaves for Free" card, turning lemons into lemonade by creating a raving fan out of someone who thought they were complaining.

The same goes for screwups on the job. They are inevitable and at the same time a golden opportunity to communicate to your clients that you care, you have their interests at heart, and you will not chisel them but rather hold the relationship as something that is precious and to be protected and invested in for the long term.

Good Intentions

You can talk about the behavior that engenders trust all day long, but in the end, it is your heart that really matters.

> If you go into it trying to sell a product or an engagement or a project singularly, I think you will fall down. It is about trust, it is about relationships, it is about caring, caring for the business, and caring for the person that really carries the day. If they can see that you care, you will earn trust.
> —Dave Smith, senior managing director, Accenture

Caring is the one thing you can't fake. It is a window into who you are. When clients feel you care, that you live your life treating others like you would like to be treated, they trust you to be their extensions into the marketplace, to advise them on their most vexing problem, and to be their agents in fixing what's wrong. *Seeing that you care is a prerequisite to trust.*

Face Time

Human beings are animals that drink in their surroundings by hearing, touching, smelling, tasting, and seeing what is around them. They take each's other measure by being with each other; indeed, there is a growing body of research that suggests that they "thin slice" judgments of each other using information gathered from all the senses simultaneously. We are fans of the phone and video conferencing, and they work to build trust as well, but building trust over phone and video takes more time than face-to-face. Sitting down and sharing a meal with a potential client is one of the oldest and most reliable ways to build trust with them. That said, don't rush things. Trust cannot be expedited. Talk on the phone once or twice, then ping them with "I'm going to be in San Diego. I'd love to put a face to a name. Are you open for lunch?"

14

Element 6: I Am Able

I've Got Budget and Buy-In

"**W**e want to do work for IBM."

Doug was having coffee with the CEO of a professional services firm that was small but growing, with a fifteen-year reputation for doing excellent work.

"We could help them. I know we could," said the CEO.

Doug looked at his Americano. He wasn't quite sure what to say. IBM did almost $80 billion in worldwide revenues while his client would be lucky to break $4 million in sales. It's one thing to ask for marketing advice, it's another to enable someone's delusion.

Despite the look on Doug's face, the client was undeterred. "We can get anyone. Watch."

Doug remembers that coffee with a smile.

He got IBM in the end, and it wasn't luck. It was pure, distilled perspiration. They worked it. I remember the first thing they did was to reach out to the head of the operating group with which they wanted to work. They had an intern Google half the night until she found the guy's email address. Then they pinged the guy, but didn't get a response. But that was only the start. When that didn't work, the CEO called around to people he knew to find someone who was currently working with IBM, someone who could steer them in the right direction.

And that worked—at least partially. He found a woman with whom they had worked at a different firm. She was out on her own and was doing some consulting for a unit inside of IBM. He and his team renewed the friendship and asked for her help getting into IBM, putting her on a generous 20 percent commission. "You get us in, and we'll be happy to pay you." She was wonderful, setting up half a dozen meetings with staff members who seemed like they were in the right departments. Somehow, though, nothing ever seemed to materialize. The CEO was getting frustrated. IBM had become a kind of holy grail. He was sure what they did would be a perfect fit for how he was reading their strategy. He had absolute confidence in his ability to win work with IBM.

That's when a senior partner at the CEO's firm decided to reach out to an operating executive at IBM he'd found on LinkedIn. The guy was two or three degrees separated, but the two of them struck up a conversation online that seemed to careen back and forth between business and their common love of football. After a *year* of this kind of back and forth, the IBMer said he wanted to talk to the partner by phone. They talked business objectives, a project proposal was exchanged, and six months later my client was working for the elephant they'd been stalking for so long.

"Here's the thing," the CEO told Doug. "As hard as it was to get in, it is a good fit. We're doing good work for them and now they are expanding our mandate. Sometimes you have to keep trying until you find the right person. If we had just taken the first 'no' as their final answer, we wouldn't be helping them today." It is all about finding the right person.

Ability

Finding the right person inside a firm is an art, not an act of will or science.

Clients buy when they know who you are, know what you do, feel like what you do is relevant to their goals, think you can do the job, and trust you. But that is not enough. They also need to be able to pull the trigger and the timing needs to be right—the subjects of this chapter and the next one.

In the world of sales, the term of art for asking if a would-be client is *able* to engage with you is "prequalifying." The logic goes, "Don't spend time on dry holes. Drill a test, see if there is oil there, and only then commit resources."

Intuitively we know how prequalifying works. If you are fifty-six, have a slight stoop from too much time hunching over a laptop, have a dent where your wedding ring was, and walk into a Porsche dealership, they will let you test drive the 911. You look like the type of person who would be serious about buying a Porsche. If you are sixteen, the red dots on your face look like a constellation, and your shorts hang impossibly low on your hips, you're not going to get a test drive.

Karen Swim is a twenty-year public relations and marketing communications pro. CEO of her own firm, Words for Hire, she is a wonderful writer—able to capture the essence of a truth in pithy, well-crafted prose. In a recent blogpost, she summarizes how to size up clients before wasting too much time in conversation with them.

I prequalify every opportunity to:

1. **Evaluate if there is a real opportunity.**

   Sometimes a prospect is on a 'fishing expedition,' while other times it's obvious they won't be able to get the needed buy-in internally. Are they trying to leverage information to get a better rate from a current provider? Are they gathering information to determine if PR services are something they may have interest in implementing someday (rather than now)? In the worst cases, a "prospect" has no intention of hiring outside counsel: they're hoping an unwitting PR pro will give them ideas in a proposal they can use without paying for them. Asking probing questions initially will help you uncover a prospect's motives—if you're lucky, you'll find that they are very interested in hiring *you*.

2. **Determine fit.**

   Does the company culture align with yours? Are the expectations realistic? During this prequalification phase, prospects often give clues about how organized they are—both personally and internally within the company. You can also ask questions about their goals and how they are measured, which will tell you a lot about their internal culture and what will be expected of you.

3. **Identify if there is a budget.**

   Many independent consultants feel intimidated to ask this question, but don't be! Budget signals a commitment and allows you to determine the scope of work. "Do you have a defined budget for PR/Communication Services?" is a professional question to ask.

If the opportunity qualifies, and a proposal is requested, I move to a more in-depth pre-proposal interview—this early step ensures that a written proposal is merited. Using this process has allowed me to write fewer proposals, but with a much higher close ratio.

There's a lot of truth in what Karen has written. If would-be clients have no interest in buying, have crazy expectations, or have no money, spending too much time with them in the short run may not make a lot of sense.

Art Gensler, author of *Art's Principles* and founder of Gensler, puts it this way:

> It is important that you sit across the table from an empowered manager who can make a decision. If that individual is unable to control the selection, then enlist your original contact to be your advocate. Have that contact guide you to the right person who can make the decision.
>
> —Art Gensler, *Art's Principles*

As good as this advice is, here's the thing: ruthlessly prequalifying leads before deciding to engage with them goes completely against the idea that you should invest in your network over a lifetime and believe in a kind of karmic business model—where what you harvest is a direct function of what you sow.

In fact, we think this idea that we should prequalify buyers early-on is often wrong. Of course, would-be clients have to be able to buy from you—they have to have both authority and budget—but we have found that *engaging with people who do not have authority and budget is often the only way to figure out who does.*

Some of us have the luxury of having smaller firms as clients. With them, it is possible to sit down over coffee with the founder or CEO and cut a deal, but others also work with very large organizations that can be triple-matrixed across business lines, geographies, and functional expertise. In organizations like these, rarely can someone make a unilateral decision to engage with us. More precisely, even when they can unilaterally decide to engage with us and have the authority and budget to do so, they rarely do so because they value the advice of their colleagues and are eager to bring along partners, direct reports, and other stakeholders. In the twenty-first century, where it is axiomatic that good managers encourage wide participation across the team, decision making is either a team sport or a goat rodeo depending on the day.

> Looking back, I can see that the thing I always underestimated was how if you hire a consultant, it's a career risk. The bigger the prize, the bigger the risk. I knew it, but now I understand it on an emotional level. I understand how important it is to sell internally and not just to the person. I see how you need to sell your services to a person's colleagues in a way that it will make it palatable or understandable. I now know that if someone is thinking about hiring us, they are thinking, "How will this be accepted by the rest of the organization?"
> —Walt Shill, formerly of McKinsey and Accenture

A Miscalculation

Yes, if you offer high-end data analytics to firms who actively hedge their supply chain inputs, maybe you shouldn't be knocking on your local dry cleaners' door, plying your wares. But beyond that high altitude sift, rushing to eliminate would-be clients because technically they can't buy is a mistake. In fact, we think prequalifying companies and executives with anything other than a very wide screen is a miscalculation. Here's why:

> No one is ever able to buy your services. No one ever has budget. Not at least yet. A tight screen will eliminate them all. All of them can buy, however. They can speak to the need for budget *given a compelling enough case.*

Consider the following prequalifying conversation:

"It's been fun getting to know you. You seem like you care about supply chain analytics and are focused on optimizing your hedging strategy, which makes you unusual in our experience. At the risk of being direct, do you have budget and the authority to pull the trigger on a firm like ours?"

No need to read further. You already know the answer.

"There are others I would want to bring in on this. And, to tell you the truth, we're being asked to make cuts across the organization. Next year might look different."

Judging from that answer, does this prospect pass the pre-qualification test? No. But we'd say you'd be crazy to cross them off your list. You offer expert services. Expert services are provided to a network of people who you get to know over a lifetime. This is not software. You don't have a boss breathing down your neck measuring dials per hour and sales funnel yield. A much better question is, "Under what conditions would this prospective client be able to act?"

The Magic Formula

Universally, clients report they are able to buy when presented with high return-on-investment (ROI) propositions and when they are at the right level to rally the troops around a given opportunity. The magic formula is:

$$\text{High ROI} + \text{Right Level of Stakeholder} = \text{Ability}$$

For nearly a decade Tom worked in the private equity business as a finder. He was the dog whose job was to bring back the ducks—companies that would make good investments.

In that role, he crisscrossed the United States, earning way too many airline miles and learning a thing or two about what makes businesses tick. "If a company makes money," he says, "it can distribute that cash to shareholders or invest in growth. If a CEO decides on the latter strategy, or if she is looking for outside growth capital, she needs to understand the return dynamics inside her businesses. If you open four new stores and each cost a million dollars, the key questions are how long will it take for them to break even and begin to earn a return, and what does that return look like over time? Is it better than what her shareholders could earn in other opportunities on a risk-adjusted basis?"

Tom often hears a plaintive cry of fellow business owners in search of capital. "There's no equity funding available. All the VC and private equity firms are focused on the big cities. We need more access to capital."

He thinks this perspective is wrongheaded. In his experience, capital will bust down doors, travel great distances, and contort itself in unnatural ways in an effort to invest in high-return opportunities. For capital, the problem is not enough deals; it is the dearth of high-performing business models. Listen to what Bain says in their 2016 report on Global Private Equity.

> The difficulty of putting capital to work, combined with ongoing investor enthusiasm for the private equity asset class

has led to a new record amount of dry powder, now totaling $1.5 trillion across all PE fund types globally.

You read that right. There are 1.5 trillion dollars sitting on the sidelines, waiting to be invested in companies who can demonstrate they know how to earn strong returns on capital. Sit down for breakfast at the Peninsula Hotel in Manhattan, eavesdrop on the private equity partners nattering away as they nosh on their twenty-dollar granola parfaits, and you will hear the same thing year after year. "There are no good deals anymore. Too much capital is bleeding out all the returns."

What they are saying is that money is starved for high ROI opportunities.

It's no different in the companies we hope to serve as consultants and providers of professional services. While our clients are more likely to be working in a downtown Minneapolis office building and not supping in Manhattan on 55th and 5th, their concerns are *exactly the same*.

They don't talk about dry powder or the need for proprietary deal flow. Instead, they say, "Should I ask for budget?" and "How can I spend money that will move the needle for my company?" It is the same thing, however. It's a cry for attractive returns.

Return on Investment

ROI is a simple concept. How much money is being spent and how much does the investment earn either in profits or savings?

But in some ways, ROI is a misleading calculation. Better is to ask, "what's the rate of return?" adding the element of time.

Making a 50 percent return on money over a year is better than making it over twenty. Time makes a difference. That's why when we are talking with potential clients about helping them with our services, and they ask us about ROI, we respond by saying, "Over what period of time?"

Interestingly, the executives with whom we speak ask about ROI but then shy away from the actual math. Instead, they talk in coded language that acts like a kind of stand-in for ROI calculations. "What will my boss think?" "Will this make me a hero?" "Could I lose my job over this?" "If I don't do it, what are the costs associated with inaction?" "What are others in the industry doing?" "How will I budget for this?" Despite all this soft language, the logic driving a would-be client's ability to act on your proposal is always, "What kind of efficiencies will this effort bring or how will this increase our top line?" The logic of returns is immutable.

In a minute, we will discuss getting to the right level in an organization, but make no mistake, a high-return opportunity with very low risk will attract attention. It's the kind of thing junior people talk to their bosses about in excited voices over turkey wraps in the cafeteria and what C-suite executives call subordinates to discuss over the weekend. Trust the private equity professionals. The world is short of high-return opportunities. Craft one for your clients, and they will sprint in your direction.

The Right Level

There is no one too high or too low to speak with if your goal is to build a network over a lifetime. In any organization on any given day, there are a few people who are best positioned to champion your services to their subordinates, peers, and corporate bosses. You will need them because no one makes decisions in a vacuum.

As you target larger businesses, the decision-making power is not as clear as in smaller units. As the decision making becomes more complex, decision-making power is spread among more people.

—Troy Waugh, *101 Marketing Strategies for Accounting, Law, Consulting, and Professional Services*

There are two dangers to watch for when trying to identify who to focus on in an organization:

Shooting too low. You go to an industry conference, put on your best blue blazer, and head down to the cocktail party ready to talk it up with potential clients. Waiting to grab a drink from the bar, you start talking with a young man in a royal blue suit that rides up high enough that you can see his striped socks. You feel a little old. He is pleasant enough, though, and, as it turns out, he works for a firm you would like to work for.

What do you do?

- Prequalify him out and move on? Right firm, but wrong level.

- Chat him up, then ask him if his boss is there and would he make an introduction?

- Talk to him seriously as a peer, engage him on the future, and ask him questions on where he sees the world going. Follow up with an interesting article that is relevant to what he was saying?

The right answer is the last option. Your job is to create relationships. You have no idea where those relationships will lead. This young man with whom you are speaking could be the next CFO of a hot start-up. He might be tapped for his talent to run a division in your niche, or he might just be someone you could interview later for information. Take his card and give him a call in a week. "It was great to meet you. I am wondering if I could ask your advice. I'd love to work for you guys. Who should I be speaking with?"

Do you feel like you have worked hard enough in this world that you should only speak with peers and not have to mess with "little people"? That's crazy. We are all equal in the eyes of the market. Talent and insight win, not seniority, age, or title. Treat others as you would have liked them to have treated you. When you were twenty-six, you would have died to have a serious conversation with an experienced consultant. You would have remembered that conversation for years.

Shooting too high. Interestingly, this is a bigger problem for consulting and professional services pros. Frustrated with the politics of engaging with large complex organizations, we often seek to solve the puzzle by going to the top. That strategy, though, it is often as unsuccessful as shooting too low, as the preponderance of decision making is not in the C-suite at all but in divisions and units. Yes, your founder went to prep school with a CEO and that resulted in a new engagement, but mostly, we are selling to the "head of retail operations" or the "director of compliance." These are the problem solvers in an organization. The notion of an omnipotent leader is a myth, even if they are the CEO. All buyers exist in an ecosystem even if it is a sole proprietor going home to her husband to check on whether to spend the money on a new website or visit his parents in a month. Your job is to focus on the fact that the locus of decision making is often a group, not an individual.

Tactics—What Works

Determining whether or not a client has the ability to hire you is a high-touch task, meaning that it requires a high degree of one-on-one human interaction. This important step cannot be digitally automated, outsourced, or streamlined by an efficiency expert. It requires you to think and act a bit like an investigative journalist, asking lots of questions.

The important thing when it comes to determining a prospective client's ability to hire you is to know the important topics to think about well in advance. These thoughts are second nature to a seasoned rainmaker, happening almost subconsciously as a business relationship begins to take shape. For those new to the role of client development, these conversations can seem awkward, like you are asking someone out to a dance, but they needn't be. Clients are accustomed to having business partners ask about future engagements.

Here are a handful of key questions to keep in mind as you develop a new relationship with a prospective client:

1. Is our prospective client the right person in the organization to be speaking with? Is she responsible for the area of the organization that our work impacts or do they work with that person?

2. Do you know the others in the organization who will influence the final hiring decision? Have you met with these individuals as well?

3. Is her budget or funding capability in line with your customary fees?

15

Element 7: I Am Ready

The Timing Is Right

It was music to Jacob's ears.

"You've called us at a good time. I'm really glad you reached out."

"BAM!" Jacob wrote to John on Slack who was sitting in on the call, each of them in their respective offices, headsets on, leaning forward into the conversation. Nothing sounds better than a potential client telling you your timing for action is right.

"Let me talk to some folks around here, but we've been looking to start an initiative like this."

We're reminded of the Country Strong hit "Timing Is Everything" by Natalie Hemby and Troy Jones:

When the stars line up
And you catch a good break

People think you're lucky
But you know it's grace.

It can happen so fast
Or a little bit late
Timing is everything

When engaging with would-be clients, bad timing is an insurmountable wall, but good timing can open the floodgates to quick action.

Says Jacob, who is the chief operating officer of PIE, "I've been amazed at how quickly an organization can move when it is motivated. Money materializes out of nowhere. Approvals turn around in hours. Contracts get signed in days."

The reasons are often all over the map:

- New direction from the CEO
- A budget windfall
- The addition (or departure) of a team member
- The need to spend budget before the end of the year
- A return from vacation
- A stirring keynote speech

Frustration

As quickly as projects can develop if the timing is right, when the timing is wrong, like a country song about whisky, lost love, and a broken truck, nothing is sadder. It's frustrating to have a great conversation with someone whom you think your expertise can help, only to hear that familiar phrase, "the timing isn't right." For reasons beyond his control, he tells you, he can't move forward. He wants to engage, he assures you, but just isn't ready.

Institutional imperatives like budget cycles, stock price, and changes in leadership have conspired, he reports, to create an environment in which progress cannot be made.

This reminds us of a story about Tony Campenella. Tony is a management consultant who lives by the marina in San Francisco. We've changed his name for the purposes of this story because, as you will see, the story doesn't end well.

He said to us, "My goal is to make partner by the time I'm thirty-five. I know the path. It's well-worn. Break gravel in the mines. Do grunt work for a couple of years out of B-school, cranking out spreadsheets and PowerPoint slides. Then lead project teams. Then if I demonstrate good people skills, I'll become more client-facing, making presentations and attending to the care and feeding of customers. But that will only take me so far. If I want to be partner, I have to sell."

"How?" we asked him.

"I spoke with a senior partner to find out what had worked for him. He said, 'Make friends with the smartest people your age and stay in touch. Take them out to dinner every time you're in town. As they rise up through the ranks, they'll begin to give you more and more business.'"

"Seems like solid advice," we said.

Let's eavesdrop on an experience Tony had trying to sell his expertise.

"I pinged this woman with whom I went to business school. She was really smart and had done well in Redmond and was in charge of a product development group there. I asked her if we might catch up by phone. We did, and she explained to me that her team was trying to figure out what effect big data might have on their efforts. I asked her if it would ever make sense to have our team come in from the outside and give her an assessment. She said it might but warned me that she wouldn't be able to pull the trigger on a contract until later in the year."

"The words, 'Never leave the scene of the crime without setting the next meeting' rang in my mind. So, I asked her if I might pull together a team, fly out, and sit down with her people to get a sense of the issues they were facing so that when they were ready, we might be better prepared to engage."

"I was pleasantly surprised. She was really excited. I was pumped. *Partner*. It was going to happen. I scheduled the face-to-face for ninety minutes. Our team brainstormed before the meeting. I was very clear with everyone. We were going to demonstrate domain expertise by simply asking really intelligent questions. Maybe we would share a client story or two but there'd be no 'ask.' This was going to be the softest of sells. 'We're just there to be helpful,' I said."

"The day came; we jumped on the 6:25 Horizon flight up to Seattle, and were in their offices by 11:00. It went better than anyone could have expected. Really collegial. They were smart in their way, and we were smart in a little different way. The two teams complemented each other. You could see how together we were going to do good work."

"The last thing my friend said was 'Thank you. This was awesome. I've got some thinking to do on my end, but I'd be excited to work with you guys on this. Just give me a little time. There is a re-org going on right now, and we are deep in to the budget planning cycle, so it will be few more months.'"

"I was in seventh heaven. My first real foray into business development, and I was already winning. Better to be lucky than good, I thought."

"But it didn't work out that way. Six months later, two weeks before I'd posted a reminder to myself to check in, I read in the industry rag that our biggest competitor had engaged with her team to lead a digital transformation. I was devastated."

"It took me three weeks before I pinged my friend again. Thirty seconds after I hit send, she rang my cell. 'I meant to call,

Tony. We really liked your guys, but the other team was just in here a month ago. We have a new group president and he really thought they were sharp.' I was devastated."

Engagement with a would-be client is the coming together of two parties. For the match to work, the timing has to be right for both sides. Tony was ready to engage with his business school friend but missed the window by a few months. If he had been walking through the door when the new boss was thinking about new directions, he might have made the sale.

Just because you are in a hurry to engage with a client doesn't mean they are ready. The marketing guru Seth Godin referred to this outdated model as "interruption marketing." In a 1988 article in *Fast Company*, Seth offered this point of view:

> Marketing is a contest for people's attention. Thirty years ago, people gave you their attention if you simply asked for it. You'd interrupt their TV program, and they'd listen to what you had to say. You'd put a billboard on the highway, and they'd look at it. That's not true anymore.
>
> The interruption model is extremely effective when there's not an overflow of interruptions. If you tap someone on the shoulder at church, you're going to get that person's attention. But there's too much going on in our lives for us to enjoy being interrupted anymore. So, our natural response is to ignore the interruptions. . . .
>
> Interruption marketing is giving way to a new model that I call permission marketing. The challenge for companies is to persuade consumers to raise their hands—to volunteer their attention. You tell consumers a little something about your company and its products, they tell you a little something about themselves, you tell them a little more, they tell you a little more—and over time, you create a mutually beneficial learning relationship. Permission marketing is marketing without interruptions.

While Godin was taking aim at consumer products companies, his point is relevant to your efforts to connect with those you feel you could most serve. Your outreach is happening at a time that is convenient for you, by definition. "I think I'll send out that white paper on audit reform in Europe when the kids leave for camp. I'll have time then." Inevitably, though, when the email hits your potential client's inbox, they are busy doing the moral equivalent of eating dinner. They're about to walk into a marketing meeting in Prague, attend their son's graduation from Davidson, review their departments' board presentations, or finally have that pedunculated polyp removed from their stomach lining.

As the partners at the RAIN Group, a professional services marketing firm, say:

> As much as you might like to shorten the sales cycle, buying complex, important, trust-based services takes time. The initial lead will culminate only if the buyer, when she has a need that floats to the top of her to-do list (the elusive time of need), thinks of you.
> —Mike Schultz, John E. Doerr, and Lee W. Frederiksen,
> *Professional Services Marketing*

Bumps in the Road

We want our first interaction with a potential client to speed along like an Audi R8 on the track, but more often, it bounces along uncertainly like a 1999 Ford half ton on an uneven dirt road. Common bumps in the road include:

- *Personnel changes:*
  "I wanted to call and let you know that I will be leaving the company."

"We just got a new CEO and are on hold until we find out which direction he intends to take us."

"I'm currently trying to hire a pro on this very subject. I am going to want to get that done, consult with her or him before moving forward with you."

- *Reorganization:*

"I'm not sure if you've heard, but we are moving from a network of offices around-the-world model to more of a global-business-unit model."

"I'd want the acquisition to shake out before we move forward."

"We're in the midst of a big merger. I am not actually sure of my role going forward."

- *Business imperatives:*

"Our stock price got clobbered after that pharma pricing scandal. No one wants to do anything before we see the fallout around that . . . ."

"Our CFO just ordered 10 percent cuts across the board. None of us want to lay people off. It means there is no money for outside consultants."

"We aren't going to be making any big moves until we figure out whether or not tax reform is going to happen."

- *Priorities:*

"I love this idea, but we need to finish our global industry review first."

"We always try to make a big effort at the ACM/IEEE supercomputing conference. Let's chat after the dust settles on that."

"I've a bunch of international travel coming up. I'm frankly not sure I have the bandwidth to focus on this until the fall."

- *Substitutes:*

  "We're speaking with a number of other firms about this . . . ."

  "I've heard that Bluestream does something similar, only they survey customers as part of their methodology."

  "The money for this would have to come from our advertising budget and right now we are making a big push to support the rebranding."

- *Silent killers:*

  "I can't really talk about it now, but there're some power struggles going on around here."

  "We'll need to get buy-in from the head of research, and he generally has a bias against outsourcing."

  "We had a breach with a vendor. The CFO's nixing most consultants."

- *In-housing:*

  "This is central to our business model, and I think we should be doing this kind of work ourselves."

  "I recognize you would be arms and legs on this project, but I think I can round up some internal resources to work on this."

  "I'd like to give our team here a shot at this first before bringing in reinforcements."

- *Price:*

  "That might be a bridge too far for us . . . ."

  "Is there some way we could do a pilot?"

  "We could never make that kind of commitment. Do you ever do some kind of gain share arrangement . . . ?"

  And finally,

- *Loss of momentum:*

  "Ms. Arden needs to cancel the follow-up call, as she will be traveling then."

  "Looks like they're no-shows. Did they accept the invite?"

  "Can we revisit this in Q3?"

Tactics—What Works

You are well acquainted with each of these bumps. They have all happened to you in your business development efforts. The job of corralling people and resources to create value is not easy.

Be patient. As a consultant or professional service provider who dominates a niche, your job is to build and underwrite a conversation among experts and those who can benefit from that know-how. This is a life's work. Keep saying to yourself, "life is long," because it is, and you have no idea when the stars will align and the opportunity to collaborate will rise like Jupiter in the night sky.

Continue to serve. Remind yourself that you're not selling to would-be clients; you are helping others succeed. The money will get straightened out in time. If someone tells you they are not ready to engage, they are telling you:

- I'm aware of you.
- I understand what you do.
- I am interested in speaking with you because you are relevant to my priorities.
- I know you to be capable.
- I trust you to watch my back.

- I have the ability to act.
- *It is just that the timing of what you suggest is not quite right.*

So, don't sweat it. You are most of the way there. Just keep adding value, sending articles and links, offering to introduce them to people who could be helpful to them, including them in dinners and best practice roundtables you sponsor, and visiting them when you are in town.

Stay proximate. If you do not stay in touch, awareness of who you are fades. You gave that great presentation at AUTEX about textile reuse, but that was four years ago, and out of sight, out of mind. Count on the fact that dozens of new bright shiny objects have floated in and out of your would-be client's field of view. You have to stay in touch, whether that is through a note, drinks, or a forwarded blogpost, to stay on the top of their mind.

When a prospect doesn't hire you early, he is not rejecting you. People have different circumstances and different time-tables for making decisions.
—Troy Waugh, *101 Marketing Strategies for Accounting, Law, Consulting, and Professional Services*

Herman Ebbinghaus, the early twentieth century psychologist, devoted much of his life to trying to understand memory and forgetting. He was the first person to coin the phrase "learning curve." He found that learning is most pronounced after the first exposure to a topic and diminishes over time, with each additional exposure contributing less and less to total retention. Ebbinghaus described what we all know, namely that the first day of work is the hardest because we are being flooded with new information, which is pushing our limits to absorb it. In bad news for consultants and professional services pros everywhere, he also described the "forgetting curve," finding there is an exponential drop-off in retention over time. The worst is the first twenty minutes, though there is pronounced drop-off an hour after exposure and throughout the day.

"What was the name of that guy I met yesterday?"

Worst still was Ebbinghaus' description of what he called the serial position effect. Human beings have both a primacy and recency bias, fancy words for saying that we remember the first person we met on a topic and the last one. The women and men in the middle who penned the whitepapers, spoke at conferences, took them out to dinner, and wrote thoughtful follow-up notes are forgotten. Again, first is good, and, remembering Tony, last might be best.

Look for the moment. Often in consulting and professional services, you're selling to a large organization, with its own idiosyncratic biorhythms, including planning, budget cycles, and the Byzantine politics of who's on the rise and who's not. Stay attuned to timing, and never write off a potential client. Never forget what might be called "the first precept of expert services":

No one ever needs a consultant until they do.

Clients need advisers when they encounter an unforeseen crisis or opportunity. The key word here is "unforeseen." They won't see a need to engage with you when you first meet them because they have no idea what is about to hit them. When the storm does roll in, however, they will be looking for an umbrella. It's the professional who has invested in a relationship and who is most proximate to the opportunity who wins the day. *Stay in touch.*

Burning Platforms

Daryl Conner has been in the business of change management for decades and is the author of a number of well-received books on managing through periods of change, including *Managing at the Speed of Change*. He invented the term "burning platform," a metaphor for how exogenous forces can create urgency around the need to act.

> At nine-thirty on a July evening in 1988, a disastrous explosion and fire occurred on the Piper Alpha oil-drilling platform in the North Sea off the coast of Scotland. One hundred and sixty-six crew members and two rescuers lost their lives in what was [and still is] the worst catastrophe in the fifty-year history of North Sea oil exploration. One of the sixty-three crew members who survived was Andy Mochan, a superintendent on the rig. From the hospital, he told of being awakened by the explosion and alarms. Badly injured, he escaped from his quarters to the platform edge. Beneath him, oil had surfaced and ignited. Twisted steel and other debris littered the surface of the water. Because of the water's temperature, he knew that he could live a maximum of only twenty minutes if not rescued. Despite all that, Andy jumped fifteen stories from the platform to the water. When asked why he took that potentially fatal leap, he did not hesitate. He said, "It was either jump or fry." He chose possible death over certain death. Andy jumped because he felt he had no choice—the price of staying on the platform was too high. While listening to [this] story, I began to hear elements . . . that reminded me of what we heard when interviewing. . . . There were many parallels.

Consistently, executives said something like, *"I had to make the changes work, no matter how difficult or frightening the process was."*

Daryl's expertise is in how organizations change. His insight was that organizations change when they have to—when they have to "jump or fry." He is very clear, however, that this does not suggest one should create a narrative around potential threats in order to create demand for change. "[One] of the most prevalent misconceptions about [the idea of a burning platform is that] leaders should intentionally manipulate information or circumstance to manufacture the appearance of urgency when that's not actually the case."

And yet, this is a common belief among consultants and professional service providers. Their view is that the way to push would-be clients into being ready is to create urgency.

"Eighty-seven percent of colleges and universities have been successfully sued for employee–student sexual harassment. What sort of training do you have in place to protect against that?"

"Block chain technology will radically change the way taxes are prepared. Are you prepared for that change?"

Hawking "burning platforms" of this sort to catalyze action in a client is the opposite of being a trusted advisor who is committed to a client's best interests over the long haul. So how do you bring up risk you might see for a client? Start from the specifics of their company and build up to the conclusion rather than moving from the general to specific. "We see your SEO is not optimized and that you are missing, by our estimate, 40 percent of available traffic. We can help you capture those eyeballs." That is better than, "Ninety-three percent of all commercial websites are being out-competed by rival sites that optimize search words. Is your site optimized?" One is a statement of fact. The other is a manipulation.

One of the enduring challenges of running a consulting or professional services firm is projecting revenues. It doesn't matter if leadership charges the account planning teams with 10 percent growth; knowing *with certainty* when a client is going to ripen into a new engagement is an exercise in seeing around corners. One friend of ours who is a senior partner at Bain and who consults large companies on strategy said, "This is a feast-or-famine business. On a good day, you have visibility over the next six months. Nothing more. It's why layoffs are endemic to the industry."

In the face of ambiguity in the marketplace, there is only one defense. Do good work, make new friends, build your network, and have faith that companies have an embedded desire for value over time. In fact, they are hungry for it. They may not be ready to embrace that value right now, when you are out stopping by and saying, "Hi," but in the long run, the kind of true value you bring with your expertise and experience is magnetic. It just might take a while because, as the country song says, "timing is everything."

Putting the Seven Elements to Work

16

A Chain Is as Strong as Its Weakest Link

Using the Seven Elements as a Diagnostic Tool

Tom used to bake bread when he was at Great Harvest. He remembers there was something simultaneously loose and tight about a recipe. With bread, you can add cranberries and walnuts, or cracked pepper and parmesan cheese. You can swap out whole wheat flour for rye, and you can substitute molasses for honey. The variations are endless.

At the same time, you need to follow a recipe closely, or you'll end up with a gummy, tasteless mess on your hands. Turns out that while they are platforms for creativity, recipes describe what's both necessary and sufficient to make bread and are, as such, unforgiving. They do four things. They tell the baker which ingredients must be put in the bowl to produce bread. They speak to the order in which those ingredients must be combined, they tell the baker how much of each ingredient to use, and finally they describe the processes—stirring, kneading, proofing, and baking—that must be performed.

Bread, in its simplest form, is made up of five ingredients: flour, yeast, salt, water, and something sweet. This is what business school–types call a mutually exclusive, collectively exhaustive (MECE) list of ingredients—each are separate from the other and together they are both complete and necessary. There is no vagueness or overlap between the ingredients. Nothing essential has been left out.

We set out in this book to share the seven elements of *how clients buy*. We believe that in consulting and professional services, you do not win new business by focusing on sales funnel–type activities but rather by starting from a place of empathy with your would-be clients. This empathy requires us to view the buying journey from the perspective of what prospective clients need before they can engage and only then to ask, *"How can I support a potential client as they seek to satisfy these seven basic needs?"*

Think of it as a strategic business development recipe. Making sure a prospective client's seven basic needs are met is like making sure you get all the essential ingredients in the bowl.

- If a client needs to be **aware** of you before engaging, what is the best way to ensure that they know you exist?
- If a client needs to **understand** what you do, how could you best explain your specialty?
- If a client needs to be working on their priorities, how can you help connect your capabilities and their goals? How can you connect with their **interest**?

- If a client needs to know you are capable of doing the work, how could you assure them? What will be the ground of **respect** on which your relationship is built?

- If a client needs to **trust** that you have their best interests at heart, how can you build a relationship characterized by trust?

- If a client needs the authority to pull the trigger, how can you support them by building the internal case and giving them the **ability** to engage?

- If a client needs to act when they are **ready**, how can you make sure you are there when they need help the most?

The Right Measure: Three Types of Service Firms

Recipes speak to more than MECE elements; they include recommendations on proportion. For example, a recipe tells us how much honey we should add to activate and feed the yeast. It's the same for how the seven elements work to help you grow your practice. Just as the proportion of ingredients may change with different bread recipes, the proportion of emphasis on the different elements will vary depending on what type of service you provide.

In our experience, independent of whether you work in law, accounting, or management consulting, there are three categories of professional service firms—*evergreen, acute, and optimizing.* Let's start with a high-level description of each:

a. *Evergreen.* These service providers work with clients year-in and year-out. An example is an accountant who specializes in tax preparation, or a human resources consultant who vets and performs background checks on all new employees.

b. *Acute.* These specialists come to the rescue just in time. Think of a tax attorney specializing in estate planning, a turnaround consultant that specializes in Chapter 7 bankruptcies, or a divorce attorney for high net-worth individuals. Their engagement with clients is not recurring over time, but rather episodic based on need, often urgent.

c. *Optimizing.* These service providers help clients get better at a specific aspect of their business; typically helping increase revenue, minimize cost, or reduce downside risk. They may improve one's intranet security, buttress one's growth strategy, or optimize a global supply chain. They are different from acute providers in that engaging them is discretionary. There is not an emergency they are responding to. We need to update our website. We could do this today or after the holidays depending on cash flow.

Understanding which of the service categories you are in can help you focus on the most important elements for your category. While all seven of the elements are important, we have observed that there are certain critical elements that drive engagement with each specific service type.

	Awareness	Understanding	Interest	Respect	Trust	Ability	Readiness
Evergreen	x					x	
Acute		x		x			
Optimization			x				x

- **Evergreen** service firms provide services that are offered on an ongoing—or cyclic—basis—for example, tax professionals. Most every company hires an accountant to prepare their taxes each year. It's not a matter of *if* they engage with a CPA; it's a matter of *who*. Because of the standardized nature of recurring work, it can often be hard for evergreen providers to differentiate themselves from the competition. The challenge is either to hold on to long-time clients or to boot an incumbent. This is why you often hear accounting firms complain about competing on price and how responding to RFPs is a "race to the bottom."

To us, evergreen providers need to be laser focused on making sure clients *know* and *trust* them. This is why you see so many local accounting partners serving on volunteer boards as treasurers. They are trying to introduce themselves to new buyers and to work shoulder-to-shoulder with those whom they might serve. On the other hand, elements such *as interest* and *readiness* are typically not as challenging for evergreen firms. Generally, what evergreen firms do is easily understood, and the presumption is that as CPAs they are well qualified. The main question a client has is, "Do I know you?" and "Will you have my back and safeguard my interests?"

- **Acute** service firms are brought in on short notice to solve an emergency. These are firms that specialize in crisis management, bankruptcies, system crashes, PR disasters, and turnaround situations. The critical elements for acute service providers are *understanding* and *respect*. Their challenge is to clearly articulate their niche (do you do exactly what I need?) and establish a high level of credibility (are you the best?) so when an emergency hits, they are top of mind.

  Acute service providers need to be in the trade news letting people know about every fire they put out. They also need to cultivate their network of intermediaries because it is generalists who often refer clients to specialists. "We can't help you with this, but we have often sent clients to Jones Hatchett and we hear good things back." "I don't do divorces, but Janice Schaefer is excellent at this type of work."

Acute specialists typically don't need to worry as much about available funds (e.g., ability) or readiness. If there is an acute need, clients will usually find the authority and budget. Because the trigger event hits such a small percentage of the population at any time (if ever) and the timing is unpredictable, acute providers typically cannot afford to do much in terms of direct business development. Mass advertising is far less useful than networking with those who can refer them to prospective clients.

- **Optimizing** service firms frequently have the hardest sell of all as their services are usually optional. For example, in an effort to stay in shape, you might maintain a gym membership (an evergreen service). If you got really sick, your doctor might refer you to a specialist (an acute service), but under what conditions would you hire a personal trainer? When it was important to you. For some reason, your priorities change, and suddenly you are prioritizing the decision to add extra help to your approach to fitness. What was a *"No, I'm not interested,"* becomes, *"When can we get started?"*

  Optimizing service providers struggle to uncover *interest* in would-be clients because what they do is optional. Optimizers spend a lot of time working to establish *interest* and to be present when priorities and *readiness* changes. Many old pros in the consulting and professional services business will tell you that the secret to business development is to ask lots of questions. They see questions as the key that unlocks the consultative sale, and they are correct. Questions play a particularly important role for optimization firms because it is in the answers to questions that would-be clients reveal the problems they are interested in tackling and for which the timing is right. This process of discovery is far more important than it is for evergreen or acute firms where the problem is familiar or obvious.

Using the Seven Elements as a Diagnostic Tool

Like a recipe, the seven elements can also be used as a diagnostic tool. If you pull bread from the oven and it is a hot mess, you naturally want to know what went wrong. Did you leave out the salt? Was the oven turned up too high? Likewise, maybe your practice spends hundreds of thousands on advertising at a major conference, yet nothing seems to come of it. You find yourself asking, "do prospective clients understand exactly what area of HR we specialize in?" Maybe you're getting lots of interest from potential clients, but you're not closing enough deals. Could it be a credibility issue? Have you shared enough compelling case studies? Maybe you are writing lots of proposals but are consistently losing to competitors. Could it be you need to work more on building trust and investing in relationships over the long term?

The seven elements framework provides a useful and consistent vocabulary to discuss business development opportunities within your own organization. When you sit down with your team and talk about how you are reaching out to those you are interested in serving, there are three levels where you can put the Seven Elements to work.

1. *From the perspective of the client.* Whether you are doing account planning on your largest customer (How can we expand our mandate?) or looking over a list of companies with whom you have never worked (How could we begin to engage with them?), it's helpful to use the seven elements as a scorecard.

   - Awareness: Who else in the client's organization needs to know who we are?

   - Understanding: Do they know what we are really good at doing?

   - Interest: Do we have a sense of their priorities?

- Respect: Do they have objective proof of our capabilities?
- Trust: Have we spent the time to communicate that we will always put their interests first?
- Ability: Are we talking to the right person who has the authority to engage?
- Readiness: Are we staying close to them over time so they reach out to us when their need materializes?

2. *From your personal perspective.* Maybe you are a partner in a large firm or a new sole proprietor trying to establish a name for yourself. What are you doing to build awareness with those you wish to serve? Or perhaps you're a senior partner that is pivoting to a new service niche. What are you doing to establish your personal credibility and respect on the emerging topic? The seven elements can provide a useful framework of thinking through your top action items.

3. *From the perspective of the firm.* How solid is your firm's brand reputation? If you're a one hundred-year-old regional law firm with a reputation of being smart, honest, and dependable, awareness may not be an issue. Conversely, if you are a new web development startup with three employees, getting your name out in the marketplace may be a top priority. If you're the chief marketing officer of a global HR consultancy, what are your top priorities in supporting your would-be clients in every step of their buying journey?

Seven Elements Self-Test

In using the seven elements as a diagnostic tool, you can use the following questions to get a sense of where you have solid, well-developed muscle and where there are opportunities to do a little work. This simple questionnaire may lead to an interesting discussion with your team or partners. Have each teammate or colleague take the questionnaire separately. Then, average the scores and compare your individual ratings.

Rate each statement from 0 to 5 to represent your level of agreement.

5 = Strongly agree

4 = Agree

3 = Somewhat agree

2 = Somewhat disagree

1 = Disagree

0 = Strongly disagree

Element 1: Awareness

- We have well-defined criteria for selecting the companies we wish to target as prospective customers.
- As a company, we have agreed upon a target list of prospective customers.
- We have a high success rate of scheduling initial contact meetings with our target audience.
- When we reach out to a potential customer, in most cases they have already heard of us.
- We make follow-up contact on a regular basis with our target customers.
- We use a variety of media formats when building awareness with our target audience. (e.g., phone, web meetings, in person, e-brochures, white papers, case studies, etc.)
- We are very good at building brand awareness with our target audience.

Element 2: Understanding

- We are skilled at presenting our message to prospective customers.
- Our prospective clients clearly understand exactly what it is that we do.
- Our prospective customers have a very good understanding of what makes our offering unique.
- Our current marketing collateral is easy to understand.
- Our current marketing materials project the brand image for which we are striving.
- We use a variety of media formats to clearly articulate what we do.

Element 3: Interest

- We research our prospective customers to ensure our services are relevant to them.
- Before reaching out to a prospective customer, we think carefully about whether our service will have a significant impact on their business goals.
- We listen carefully to our clients to understand their unique business needs.
- We clearly explain how we could have a compelling impact on a prospective client's business.
- After our first introductory meeting, our prospective clients show a high degree of interest in learning more about what we do.

Element 4: Respect

- We clearly outline to each prospective client the specific benefits of the work that we do.

- We proactively identify the potential risks that a prospective client might perceive in working with us.
- We are skilled at addressing perceived concerns a prospective client might have about working with us.
- We are prepared to answer questions about how our process is better than our competitors'.
- We provide a trial offer or a guarantee to alleviate any concerns a prospective new client might have about working with us.
- Our clients fully understand the ROI of the work we do complete with projected financial benefits and costs.
- By the time we present a proposal, our clients are confident that we can deliver on the work that we say we can do.

Element 5: Trust

- We are totally honest in our working relationship with prospective clients.
- Our prospective clients perceive us to be highly dependable.
- We demonstrate to our prospective clients that we have their best interests in mind at all times.
- By the time we get to the proposal phase, our prospective clients feel completely comfortable working with our team.
- I believe that our prospective clients completely trust us.
- We have a number of references that will speak highly about working with us.
- We are good at cultivating potential clients over time and continue to add value over the course of many months.

Element 6: Able

- We assess early on whether a prospective client has the funding available to hire us.
- We are rarely surprised to find that our prospective client is not the final decision maker on a project with us.
- We are proactive in getting support for our work from a prospective client's key organizational stakeholders.

Element 7: Ready

- We pay close attention to our prospective client's organizational climate to understand if the "timing is right" for working with us.
- When a prospective client isn't interested or ready to engage with us, we patiently and persistently continue to build the relationship.
- We are very effective at staying in touch with prospective clients so that we are top-of-mind when the timing is right for them to engage with a service provider.

What patterns do you see? What are your strengths? Weaknesses? Where do you feel you are putting most of your energy? What are you not emphasizing? Where are deals getting hung up?

To benchmark your answers with others, go to https://howclientsbuy.net/assessment.

Focus on Where You Need to Improve

Practices often reflect the strengths of their leaders. If you are a natural relationship builder, you will emphasize that. If you think drinks and dinner are the key to relationships, that is what you will do. But know that looking at your practice using the seven elements and grading yourself and your firm objectively can provide important insights that can result in shoring up your practice where you may be weak.

- You do a great job asking for referrals but don't have a website. People have started to comment to you about how a web presence is table stakes these days, but you hate everything about websites—the design, the messaging, the techno-jargon around functionality. Then it occurs to you. I'm a consultant. Maybe I should hire a consultant to lead me through the process of setting up a website.

- Technology drives your practice. You use a demand-generation software to push out blogs and whitepapers, tracking downloads and time spent. The technology works pretty well, but you often find yourself stumbling through what should be an easy conversation with would-be clients. You just don't have the ability to express what you do well. Even though you can do the work, you just can't explain it. You see the work that is being lost and ask a colleague who is good at explaining your work to begin to drive those calls, using you as a subject matter expert.

- For many years, you were willing to take on any work from any client, but a review of your last two years of projects shows that increasingly your new business is coming from customer experience executives in regional banks. You decide to aggressively niche yourself to become the go-to expert in this emerging market.

- The world seems so big. You just opened the new office in San Francisco. You look out of your office in the Embarcadero and see what looks like millions of possible clients. You've been advertising in the trade publications. People have a good sense of what you do, but actually sitting down with decision makers is proving to be difficult. You realize you need to find a better way to build rapport with those you wish to serve. You sponsor a series of industry roundtables with the very people you hope to serve, giving them a chance to talk best practices and, at the same time, positioning yourself as a trusted advisor and someone with whom they are in regular contact.

The Myth of Likeability

In interviewing young people in consulting and professional services firms, we often heard about the need to be liked. "I think clients work with people they like." If this were true, it would present many of us with a real problem. In order to increase your practice's revenues, you would need to tune up your likeability, which seems like trying to be taller. Maybe we are just who we are. If you try to be something you're not, people will pick up on that.

The good news is that we don't think clients buy on likeability at all. We think it's a myth.

We think clients buy when they meet someone they think would add to what they are trying to do. To test this hypothesis, we asked ourselves if it was possible for us to engage with a provider that we respect and trust but do not like. The answer was yes. The easy example is the surgeon in the emergency room. We take a tumble on the slopes and break our tibia. Rushed to the hospital in an ambulance, we are wheeled into the operating suite (but only after they ask for our insurance information). The doctor comes in and begins to go to work. Our only concern is whether she is focused on her work and has seen this sort of thing before. We don't care a whit if she's nice.

For us, "like" is, at best, a tiebreaker. If you go up against another practitioner and you seem equally qualified, capable, and trustworthy, we might go with the consulting or professional services partner we like better, but only at the margin. It would be a mistake to think "like" is all there is to driving business development and an even worse mistake to write off business development misses as being because "they must not have liked us." "Like" trails far behind the engines of interest, respect, and trust.

17

Getting to Work

Learning to Think and Act like a Rainmaker

Most young professionals realize early in their careers that, at some point, skill in generating business will be an important determinant of their success.

—David Maister, "Young Professionals: Cultivate the Habits of Friendship"

Our primary goal in interviewing accomplished professionals in the world of consulting and professional services was to better understand how clients buy. But over the course of our interviews, we were struck by how similar their advice was to others when asked about what they would recommend to someone trying to build their practice. Here are their greatest hits in no particular order:

Do Great Work

> The key to business development is doing great work for your clients.
> —Sarah Arnot, CEO, SA Leadership Performance
> (formerly with Accenture and Stuart Spencer).

Our rainmakers gave the advice, "Do great work," more than any other.

Selling professional services is different from selling a tangible product. It is impossible to separate the product from the person. In professional services, we *are the product*. If our product isn't good, no amount of marketing effort will make us successful. Even sloppy practitioners may be successful at fooling a prospective client once, but in the long run, we live by our reputations. Those with stellar reputations ultimately outcompete those with inferior reputations. In professional services, it's impossible to be a great rainmaker without having a reputation for doing great work. Your reputation will precede you. Therefore, "doing great work" must be a top priority for each professional. As Tony Castellanos, global account lead partner and industries leader at KPMG says, "The highest form of business development is delivering quality in everything you do."

But if doing great work were all that one had to do to become a rainmaker, wouldn't more professionals be great rainmakers? There are lots of talented, smart professionals with deep expertise at their craft, but less common are skilled rainmakers.

"Doing great work" isn't sufficient as a stand-alone business development strategy. It's a necessary but insufficient part of success. To be successful at developing a thriving practice in any profession, there are other important components.

Become Your Own Chief Revenue Officer

January 1, 2017 was an important day in the legal career of Chuck McDonald, a seasoned attorney in Columbia, South Carolina, with twenty-five years of experience, much of that as an equity partner. Chuck had gone to bed on New Year's Eve an attorney with Robinson, McFadden and Moore, PC and awoke the following morning an employee of Sowell Gray Stepp & Laffitte, LLC. Or, as the firm was known locally, Sowell Gray.

Three months earlier, the merger of the two firms had been announced in the local news as a joining of equals. But for Chuck, it didn't feel that way, as he saw his offices closed and the venerable name of Robinson tossed aside.

When we caught up with Chuck, he'd recently departed Sowell Gray, having decided to start his own practice. As you might imagine, he was acutely aware of the importance of being his own rainmaker, even as he seemed genuinely excited and optimistic about his future prospects.

Based on a lifetime of experience, Chuck felt strongly about the need to take responsibility for one's own business development.

> I will relay what an older lawyer who worked for a large firm once told me: "Always practice like you're the solo guy in the storefront on the street." Meaning, build your practice and develop your clients and if you do that, it allows you great flexibility and freedom. If you are dependent upon others for client generation or business coming your way, you're beholden to others. So that resonated with me, and that's what I've passed along to others: that no matter how big the firm, you have to build your own practice and develop our own client base. And if you don't do that, then you're just vulnerable.

There are lots of different personal styles of business development, and it is important to have your own unique style, but it is more important to be actively involved and proactive. Delegate business development to others at your own risk.

That said, being your own chief revenue officer doesn't mean that you aren't a team player or that you must work solo all of the time. In some professions, such as management consulting, new client opportunities are often pursued in a team environment. Reflecting on his time at A.T. Kearney, Arthur Chung said,

> I always thought that you have to do business development all on your own. The fact of the matter is that with collaboration, people can achieve similar goals. In consulting, lone wolves are very, very rare. They are out there, but I would say for the most part I feel like most partners and principals ally and work together to sell work.

Independent of what profession you work in or what stage of your career you are at, it is clear from our rainmakers that it is never too early to begin taking responsibility for business development. Clearly, as a senior partner, you're going to have more ownership of your business development than a recent college graduate. That said, now is the time for young professionals to begin laying the groundwork for future success.

Build Your Network

> The thing that I learned later in my career that I'd pass along to somebody up and coming, is never underestimate the value of networking and the value of your network. And, when I say network, I don't mean how many people you're connected to on LinkedIn. [It's] not just collecting business cards and saying, "I met somebody," but actually getting to know

them well enough that you can call up and ask a favor. That you know enough about what they're doing so you can maybe send them an article they would find interesting and really value. I think the key thing is networking, making personal connections, and recognizing that there's a lot of value there.

—Ed Keller, chief marketing officer, Navigant Consulting

Clients hire people that they know, respect, and trust, or who come highly recommended by a friend or colleague whom they know, respect, and trust. This logic implies that the more people you *know*, the more opportunities you'll have for building *respect* and *trust*. Rainmakers tend to *know* a lot of people, but it is not the number that matters—it is the quality of those relationships.

Frans Cornelius, former chief marketing officer at Randstad Holding NV and managing director at Comarco BV, understands firsthand the power of relationships. When we spoke with Frans from his office in the Netherlands, he offered this insight:

In my consulting practice, new business starts with a connection I have with the person. I have tried it the other way, trying to do business and creating the relationship later, but it doesn't work. If you don't have a good relationship, you are just one of one hundred people dancing around the problem.

Over and over we heard from the pros that it was the quality of relationships that made the difference. We've worked with Dr. Nate Bennett, a highly regarded professor at the J. Mack Robinson College of Business at Georgia State University. Nate is sought out by a number of global firms as an advisor, many of them professional services firms, and he tells us, "It needs to be a heck of a lot closer than 'we're connected on LinkedIn, and I buy you an occasional coffee.'"

It's important to note that the term "networking" has a negative connotation for some, almost in the same vein as calling what we do "selling." To some, networking implies the superficial glad-handing that occurs at some business events.

Peter Bryant, managing director at Clareo, is typical:

> I hate the word networking. [Business development is] about connecting and building relationships and nurturing those relationships in a genuine way.

But what if you're not terribly gregarious by nature, more on the introverted side, and find building and nurturing relationships difficult? Many of us in the professional services fall into this camp. Consultants, accountants, engineers, and attorneys are cerebral by nature and not generally the life of the party. Does one's tendency toward introspection imply less future success at building a professional network? According to our rainmakers, the answer is, "no." There is not one personality type that is best when it comes to business development. The key is being true to one's natural gifts.

Some professionals are really good at cold calls to individuals they think they can help. Some are strong thought leaders and enjoy writing about industry trends. Some enjoy speaking at conferences, and others enjoy meeting "new friends" at industry social events.

Dominic Barton of McKinsey stressed this point.

> One of my early mentors built his network through writing. He had perspectives on where the industry was going and what he thought needed to be done. People would call him from his writing. And he wrote a lot, and through his writing established a reputation and then a network where he was always busy. Another mentor of mine would call up new CEOs he didn't know, but felt he had some important knowledge about their situation. He would call them up

and say "Look, I'd like to talk to you because I've got some news on what you might be thinking about, or should be thinking about, or I'd like to have a discussion." I believe everyone has their own model of how they build a network. I think it's got to fit your own style. I think you've got to figure out your own approach that you're comfortable with.

Develop Your Own Style

Because we're never formally taught how to think about business development, it is natural for us to want to copy other successful rainmakers. While it may feel natural, copying another's business development approach is ultimately ineffective.

> As you develop in your professional career, it's important to not try to be something you're not. You have to understand what you are, how you do it, what makes you successful, and then don't try to be something you're not.
> —Don Scales, CEO, Investis

The veterans we interviewed told us, "To thine own self be true." No two individuals are alike, and therefore no one business development style is right for everyone.

Peter Bryant says:

> Never copy anyone. Everybody has their own style. Too many people get caught up with, "I need to be like that person." It's really understanding what are the principles by which these people operate and then adapting that to your own personal style and that's what will make you successful. I think if you try and force something, then it kind of looks awkward and disingenuous and that's when you [see] Mr. or Mrs. Slickity Slick, right? You become robotic.

Dedicate Time for Business Development

Cliff Farrah is an early riser. By the time most of us get into the office, Cliff has already called a couple of his clients and spoken with his senior leadership team about the day's events. But he lives what most would consider to be a balanced life. He regularly makes time for his family and time on the water, sailing and racing. As president and founder of The Beacon Group, a successful growth strategy consulting firm headquartered in Portland, Maine, Cliff feels an enormous personal obligation to each of his fifty-five employees:

> When I hired my first employee sixteen years ago, it was a huge milestone. And when I hired and relocated my first director and her family across the country to Portland, that changed everything for me. Now I had an obligation to that employee and her entire family.

Cliff Farrah started in the trenches after business school at A.T. Kearney. Cliff is the only consultant who ever worked directly for David Maister in Boston. Starting in the 1980s at Harvard Business School and continuing in private practice until his retirement in 2009, Maister was widely acknowledged as the world's leading authority on the management of professional services firms. Maister's classic best-selling books, like *Managing the Professional Service Firm* (1997) and *The Trusted Advisor* (2000), provided a generation of professionals with practical advice on leading their firms. Having a boss, mentor, and friend like David Maister is as good as it gets in this profession.

The skill that Cliff's closest colleagues admire most about him is his disciplined approach to business development. To some, it appears that Beacon's success comes without effort. What they don't see is the time and attention to detail that Cliff puts into growing the business. He dedicates time every day to building genuine relationships with clients and prospective clients.

> Business development is not an event, and it's not a "sometimes" thing. It is a process that I spend time on every day. If you want your firm to be consistently successful, you have to make a personal commitment to working at it each day.

For Cliff, success is not just calling on prospective clients, but developing the capability of his staff in the art of selling Beacon's strategy consulting services. Cliff's consistent daily dedication to his clients and prospective clients has paid off handsomely. The Beacon Group has grown at over 20 percent per year for nearly two decades.

For many of us, business development ebbs and flows. When work is slow, we'll fire up the business development machine and crank away until we land a project or two. Once we get busy again, we shift our attention to the work at hand. Doing quality work is vitally important, but not to the exclusion of making time for future client relationships. The most successful rainmakers make business development a consistent priority, it is part of every work week, and their success is the proof of this commitment.

Stay Persistent and Positive in the Face of So Many "No's"

Business development is one of the most challenging (and sometimes maddening) things you will ever have to do in your professional life. It's hard. Like when you know a prospective client needs help, you know you're highly qualified to do the work, you've worked hard to build the relationship and demonstrate your capability, and then the client hires someone else.

> The thing is to be persistent. Have somebody you can talk to that can continue to encourage you. You have to have thick skin because you're going get a heck of a lot of "no's" or "not interested," and you can't take them personally. You have to figure out how to motivate yourself, stay up, and stay positive, because, I will tell you, I know several people that this has just bottomed them out.
>
> —Jane Pierce, founder of Pierce Development Group
> and former VP of talent and organization
> development at ADM and Chevron

The hurdles of business development were wonderfully captured in a famous 1958 McGraw-Hill ad where a grumpy old man dressed in a business suit sits in a wooden office chair. The caption reads:

> I don't know who you are.
> I don't know your company.
> I don't know your company's product.
> I don't know what your company stands for.
> I don't know your company's customers.
> I don't know your company's record.
> I don't know your company's reputation.
> Now, what was it you wanted to sell me?
> Moral: Sales start before your salesman calls.

Walt Shill shared with us this story:

> When I was running a startup in my previous job and we were raising money, there was one fund that I thought was a perfect match; it invested in other companies like ours, and we knew some of the same people. I sent numerous emails,

but I could not get through. It took forever. And so, when I finally met the guy and the meeting goes really, really well, I said, "Steve, I have to ask you, why did it take so long to get a meeting with you?" He said, "Oh I just wanted to know if you were serious. If you don't have the persistence to call me eight times, you'll never win in this business."

Being persistent and staying positive is a trademark of all successful rainmakers.

Whatever You Do, Don't Call It "Selling"

During our conversations with senior rainmakers, we inadvertently struck a very sensitive nerve with some individuals in identifying our book's topic as "selling" professional services. To some, the term "selling" gave them great discomfort.

One of the rainmakers we spoke with in writing this book, a partner at McKinsey said,

> Selling to me gives me the heebie-jeebies. To me, the notion of selling the types of services that a consultant provides [is wrong]. You do have to generate revenue to stay in business, but if you think about it from your client's perspective, it's not about selling. It's more about solving the problem. And it's about making sure that however you're compensated for solving that problem, it produces a significant economic benefit to them.

So never say "sell." Instead commit yourself to the idea that your job is to identify a community of companies and executives to which you would like to be of service and then do everything you can to help connect those in that industry with introductions, smart articles, and peer meetings. Along this road to being of service, you will find yourself being called a rainmaker.

18

All Business Is Local

From the Silk Road to the Information Superhighway

On difficult days—the days when no one wants to speak with us, meet with us, or return our calls—we are tempted to wax nostalgic about doing business in the good old days. We harken back to when the banker and the equipment dealer knew every farmer within a fifty-mile radius. Getting heard today in a maddeningly noisy global marketplace can seem ridiculously hard.

Surprisingly, though, this is not purely a twenty-first century problem. Open since 1455, the Grand Bazaar in Istanbul, Turkey, attracts over 250,000 shoppers every day of the year (except on religious holidays) in search of bargains on everything from clothing to jewelry to rugs to food and groceries. The frenetic backdrop of haggled prices shouted back and forth colors each purchase. The Bazaar is a crazy tangle of four thousand shops underneath sixty-one covered streets vying for your attention. With so much competition, vendors often resort to aggressive tactics to get the attention of passers-by before they disappear into the next vendor's shop. For example, a carpet dealer may try to guess your nationality in an attempt to get you to stop walking. Or he may attach himself to you at the Blue Mosque to be your unofficial guide for the day.

Standing out in the global economy of expert services can seem as daunting a task as trying to sell carpets in the Grand Bazaar, but don't despair.

Despite the 24/7/365 global nature of shopping on the Internet, former Speaker of the House Tip O'Neill's adage that "All politics is local" applies to business as well. Doug likes to tell his university students that "business is a social sport." As social animals, we prefer to hire those we know. That said, just because commerce is local doesn't mean that it isn't global at the same time. It sounds contradictory, but it's not. Take the Silk Road, for example.

Long before the Grand Bazaar, there was the 4,350-mile east to west route known today as the Silk Road. According to historians, the Silk Road routes began about 200 BC and eventually connected eastern Asia with India, the Middle East, and Africa, and finally Europe. The reason the Silk Road existed was commerce, but along the way, cultures, languages, religions, and technologies were exchanged as well. The Chinese traded with Indians, the Persians with the Greeks, and the Romans with the Turkmens. They sold silk, spices, vegetables, fruit seeds, horses, rugs, clothing, and jewelry. Metaphorically, the Silk Road was the first Internet—connective tissue that linked peoples across geography.

Despite the fact that the Silk Road may have been the first glimmer of what would become a global economy, all commerce was conducted locally between people who knew each other, village-by-village and city-by-city. If you wanted to trade your Indian cardamom for silk from China, you traveled to the next village and traded with people you respected and trusted, who in turn, did the same thing one stop up the road. Your cardamom would be passed up the trade routes like an Olympic flame handed from one torch bearer to the next until it found an ultimate consumer.

Today, with a credit card and access to the Internet, we can go online and buy a rare book from a bookstore in India, or a handmade merino sweater from a vendor in Tibet. But when it comes to hiring an architect, an HR specialist, or a web developer, we typically look to people that are at best two or three degrees separated from ourselves. This is one of the reasons why global service firms spend considerable sums of money on networks of offices around the world. These firms know, instinctively, that they need to be close to their clients. Or, as a proxy, they must be willing to spend a lot of time on a phone or an airplane.

Take AECOM, for example. AECOM may not be a household name, but you know their work. The Los Angeles–based firm has 87,500 employees and revenue of more than seventeen billion dollars. For those of us who struggle to remember names, AECOM's founders were kind to us. AECOM is an acronym for architecture, engineering, consulting, operations, and maintenance. It is consistently voted as one of the best design, engineering, and architectural firms by those in the industry.

AECOM is a global company. A quick look at some of its projects speaks to their reach:

- World Trade Center
- Central–Wan Chai Bypass

- China National Convention Center
- Moses Mabhida Stadium
- Los Angeles Stadium at Hollywood Park
- Abu Dhabi International Airport
- Cape Town Stadium
- Hong Kong International Airport
- Delhi Jal Board Sewage System
- Brisbane City Hall
- Taizhou Yangtze River Bridge
- Barclays Center
- AT&T Stadium
- The Royal Bank of Scotland
- Logan International Airport

But like most global companies, AECOM understands that it must work through its local offices. Developers and government officials buy from those with whom they have spent time rubbing elbows. As a result, AECOM has hundreds of offices around the world, organized around five global hubs: North/South America, Europe, Asia, Middle East, and Australia/New Zealand. It has over a dozen offices in China alone, including a presence in Beijing, Chengdu, Guangzhou, Nanchang, and Shanghai. AECOM is a global company but it understands that identifying interest and building trust requires proximity to clients.

Making Sense of the Global-Local Paradox

For those of us whose work is truly global, this means we probably have to travel a bit more. It's hard for us to do all of our work from home if our clients are overseas. Eventually, we are going to have to sit down with a client face-to-face in their city.

Doug lives in Bozeman, Montana. Doug's previous firm, North Star Consulting Group, leads global employee and customer web survey projects. A boutique consultancy, it performs large online survey projects throughout North and South America, Europe, the Middle East, and Asia. The surveys are offered in Mandarin, Arabic, Portuguese, Russian, or any language you prefer. And even though North Star's work is truly global due to the reach of the Internet, the work always comes through a personal connection to someone Doug or a colleague had previously worked with or met at a global Fortune 500 company in the United States.

The good news for most of us reading this book is that our work is not typically global in nature. Consultants and professional service providers in the United States rarely work outside of their country. Furthermore, many among us work primarily on a local or regional basis. If you're an attorney in Austin, you probably do most of your work in Texas. If you're an accountant in Minneapolis, you probably do most of your work in the upper Midwest. If you're a civil engineer in Seattle, most of your work is in the Northwest. That's good news, because that means that most of your clients and prospective clients are also located in your city or region as well. Our work may be exposed to global and technological pressures, but for many of us, our clients are in our own backyard.

Most regional firms start with one office and subsequently expand outward geographically over time. For example, Billy Newsome's firm, Nexsen Pruet, is a regional law firm based in South Carolina. Nexsen Pruet started with just two attorneys in Columbia in 1945. Today, it's one of the largest law firms in the Southeast with over one hundred ninety attorneys in Columbia, Charleston, Charlotte, Greenville, Greensboro, Hilton Head, Myrtle Beach, and Raleigh. Knowing that commerce tends toward the local and personal, Nexsen Pruet expanded to be closer to those it wanted to serve.

But local can also mean more than just geography. Increasingly, global connectivity allows virtual communities of interest to spring up despite physical separation. Clean-tech executives meet in Santa Clara one year and in Copenhagen the next. In between sessions, they collaborate, learn, and share online. When one needs help, they might turn to a colleague half a world away for a referral even though that referral might end up being someone who is just down the street.

It's the new Silk Road.

The Future of Decision Making

This may be troubling news to some from the millennial generation who prefer to do business digitally and anonymously. Tom's wife, who is a residential realtor, shares the story of the young couple who actually tried to buy a home using their smart phone. Literally. Like, with a few swipes and taps of their thumb and index finger, and boom . . . they would be proud new home owners. The couple was shocked that they actually had to meet with a loan officer several weeks before sitting down and signing documents at closing.

We may one day get to a point of simply "swiping and tapping" when hiring consultants and professional service providers, but today's clients prefer to talk to us face-to-face before they hire us. Whether hiring a designer for the local YMCA's website or a global architect for the São Paolo Olympic Stadium, clients need to know us. To respect us. To trust us. Thus far, as humans, we haven't developed the capacity to form those connections digitally.

All business is local and personal. Even in the global economy.

19

Our Vision of the Future

A Roadmap for Change

For nearly fifty years, from the end of World War II to the fall of the Berlin Wall, the threat of nuclear annihilation hung like a cloud over life in the United States. Kids were taught to "duck and cover" in elementary school, protestors demonstrated against the bomb, and nearly all foreign policy attention was focused on containing the nuclear threat posed by the Soviets.

Today that seems like a kinder, gentler time.

Today we're concerned with terrorism, climate change, global cyber-security threats, disease pandemics, income inequality, mass migrations, economic dislocations, unsustainable food systems, and overpopulation.

It's enough to make you want to turn off the news.

But why this rise in global threats? Why have the challenges facing the world seemingly grown over the last fifty years?

Some argue it's because of mismanagement on the part of political leaders. "It's the rise of the alarmist left!" "It's the reactionaries on the right!" Others talk about how the media has gotten too efficient at scouring the globe for bad news. "Three-headed child in Myanmar eats mother!"

Both of these might be true, but we also see the rise of complex, thorny problems as a natural outcome of an increasingly connected world. Technology in communication and transportation broadens and flattens markets, and that makes all of our problems instantly global in scope. You pull a string in Toledo, and something jerks in Tokyo.

Boys in the Ladipo Auto Parts Market in Lagos use handcarts to push boxes of Sangsin brake pads that have just arrived by way of Dubai from the plant in China, grooving to the sounds of Drake on their iPhones. A *huaso* leaves his ranch outside of Puerto Natales, enters a Chilean hardware store, and buys a panel of heatproof plasterboard for his fireplace made from South African vermiculite so he can keep warm at night while he fattens yearlings that will be sold as specialty grass-fed beef in London's Keevil and Keevil shop in Smithfield Market.

It's no wonder our problems feel exhausting. Simply unknotting the ball of string that is our global supply chain would keep a team of experts busy for a lifetime.

In many ways, the fact that we are so strongly cross-linked across geography is a good thing. Code, news, points of view, photos, foodstuffs, new business opportunities, Facebook posts, memes, podcasts, medical cures, religious insights, exercise techniques, math equations, textile patterns, subway car specifications, office space architectural details, EU regulations, bread recipes, and love songs all flash across the globe at the speed of light. But then so do diseases, hacking techniques, carbon-burning vehicles, capital accumulations, and people who wish us ill.

Here's the thing: the proliferation of technology-fueled challenges requires human beings to bring more expertise to the table. As the world gets broader and flatter, we have to get better at connecting with those who need our help.

Our view is that embedded in all this global intercourse and the parallel rise in expertise are the seeds of peace, prosperity, and learning. When we swap what works and what doesn't with colleagues from around the world, the circle of those we know and respect grows—what we define as local or personal gets larger, creating a new geography in which war becomes untenable. Trade, too, creates strong incentives to keep the peace, tempering the hot tempers of ideology.

A Life Worth Living

Is the good life one where we enjoy a glass of Bordeaux on our back deck, sail in the British Virgin Islands, and play a round of golf at St. Andrews? Or is it one spent tackling great challenges where our talents are harnessed to good effect? Perhaps the good life is one marked by achievement and contribution? These are tough questions that we all wrestle with at some point in our lives.

Author Jim Collins says that the answer to the question, "What should I do with my life?" sits at the intersection of three things: what you love to do, your gifts, and what you can get paid for.

We have always been fans of this formulation. It's what we tell our high school and college-aged kids when they ask us about what they should do when they grow up. You love climbing mountains and are good at it? Figure out how to get paid for it. Are you great at math in a way that lets you earn big money but leaves you angry and exhausted at the end of every day? Time to switch things up.

But how about a *life worth living*? What does that look like? To this we'd propose a corollary to the Collins formula: a life worth living is one that sits at the intersection of wrestling with a difficult problem, using your best talents, and doing work that is consequential.

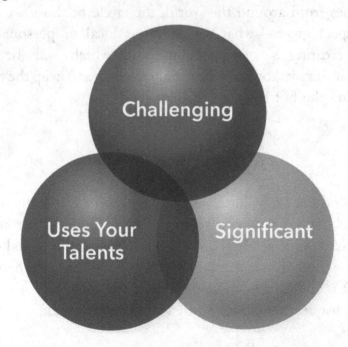

A Life Worth Living

Whenever we are working hard on something that is tough to solve and we are using our talents to their utmost in service of a problem that makes a difference in this world, we feel good. The psychologist Mihaly Csikszentmihalyi first came up with the word "flow" to describe the feeling we get when we disappear into a task. He argued this state of being fully immersed in your work is the wellspring of happiness.

> The optimal state of inner experience is one in which there is order in consciousness. This happens when psychic energy— or attention—is invested in realistic goals, and when skills match the opportunities for action. The pursuit of a goal brings order in awareness because a person must concentrate attention on the task at hand and momentarily forget everything else.
>
> —Mihaly Csikszentmihalyi, *Flow*

Irish playwright, George Bernard Shaw, offered a similar take:

> No man who is occupied in doing a very difficult thing, and doing it very well, ever loses his self-respect.

We think this is what drew many of us to the world of consulting and professional services in the first place. We like using our intelligence, education, and experience to puzzle through thorny problems that make a difference. We like the feeling of doing great work and making a difference in the lives of our clients. Our work is more than a job; it provides meaning in our lives. For a lucky few, our work is a *calling*. We are drawn to our work for reasons beyond what is simply explained by a paycheck.

In reflecting back on his first days at the Boston Consulting Group, Russell Davis remembers how honored he felt. "The chance to work at BCG was the chance to work with the smartest people at some of the world's largest companies on their hardest problems."

Important Work

You are an expert, and the world needs your expertise. Moreover, when you feel your expertise being put to work in service of important problems, it can be extremely satisfying. As Csikszentmihalyi writes, "enjoyment appears at the boundary between boredom and anxiety, when the challenges are just balanced with the person's capacity to act."

The question that brought us to write this book is "What is the best way to do business development if you are a consultant or professional services provider?" To us, "business development" means "building a bridge between an expert and those they can most help." It's the essential link between your insight and problems that need your experience and intelligence—where it can make a real difference.

For us, the world's problems make the challenge of helping smart people build a bridge to those they can help particularly urgent.

Three Imperatives for a Better Future

We began this book by saying that selling consulting and professional services is hard. It's different from selling something like a shoe or a laptop. Our services are sold on relationships, referrals, and reputation. More correctly, if we are viewing the problem from the perspective of how clients buy, we're *hired* based upon our relationships, referrals, and reputation. We pointed out a number of obstacles to us learning to become better at winning new clients. For example, we're taught to do the work but never taught how to sell the work.

We said the breakthrough for us was to abandon sales techniques borrowed from the car or software salespeople— that relentless thrash of generating leads, qualifying them, pitching, and closing. We said the secret was to stop thinking about the problem from the perspective of a salesperson whose dinner out on Saturday depends on making a quota but rather to tear a page from the world of design thinking and begin from the client's point of view—to begin from a fundamental empathy for those we most want to help.

Ultimately, we knew there had to be a better way. We hope this book has helped us get one step closer to this better way. But we know there's much work left to be done. We see the future needing progress on three important fronts:

- **Imperative 1: You**—making a personal commitment to learning the craft of business development
- **Imperative 2: Organizations**—making an organizational commitment to helping professionals learn the craft of business development in a thoughtful and ethical way
- **Imperative 3: Universities**—a substantive academic commitment to research, writing, and teaching on the topic of how clients buy

Imperative 1: You

As experts in our respective fields, we enjoy living on the edge of where knowledge ends and discovery begins. Indeed, the world looks to us to bring back what we find from our travels. It is our job to import innovation into those we serve. Let us begin to think about business development that way as well. What has worked as a way of selling materials and products is not a good fit with the burgeoning expert services economy. Yes, all business is local and personal, but the distances between trading hubs on the Silk Road are growing, and our definition of what constitutes local is expanding.

The knowledge of what works and what doesn't when we are trying to connect our expertise with those we can most help is changing all the time. Will marketing automation help or hurt our cause? Will teleconferences cut down on travel or expand markets and increase travel? Is advertising dead in a world in which the human brain is growing saturated by explosive increases in messaging? None of us really knows, which makes the field of business development an intellectual frontier.

And so this is an invitation to run toward that chaos and not away from it. Just as we are happy denizens of the edge in our professions, eagerly learning about the new and leading others as intellectual early adopters, so too we can be part of a small group that wants to learn more about how expertise connects with need. Surely the world needs this Silk Road to be wider and go to more places. Let us be the ones as individuals who embrace the challenge to create the new byways.

Imperative 2: The Organization

Second, organizations have largely left professionals on their own when it comes to their education in business development. We believe there needs to be a concerted effort by all firms—but particularly the larger elite firms—toward teaching the next generation of leaders how clients buy and how to connect with those they most wish to serve.

We have seen countless approaches to business development in the expert service industries. From our point of view, there is no one approach that is the right way. The problem is not the approach—it is the quality of the effort. We have to stop pretending that business development doesn't exist and start teaching our young professionals how to do it in effective and thoughtful ways.

Imperative 3: The University

Lastly, we believe that the time has come to study the topic of this book, how clients buy, in a meaningful way at the university level. A number of academic fields need to play a role in helping us better understand this important topic. Psychology can research the role of trust and respect in how we buy expert services. Economics can illuminate how clients decide between competing firms. Marketing can help us better understand the role of social media in how we establish a person or firm's brand reputation. Sociologists might help us understand how millennials behave differently than today's corporate leaders as it relates to hiring professionals. Will digital natives lean more heavily on online sources when making decisions, or does the need for human connection transcend one's generation?

We believe that universities will step up to study these topics; maybe not this year or next, but hopefully in the coming decades. As the saying goes, "When the student is ready, the teacher will appear." We believe the student is ready. We know that academic institutions move at the speed of glue, but over time, change can occur. Our hope is that one day there will be extensive course offerings for university students to help them better understand the topic of how clients buy.

How Clients Buy

The people we help mostly don't do what we do.

If you are a trademark attorney, the general counsel in one of your client companies doesn't register trademarks. She manages you. You do the work. That's why she hired you.

If you design tract housing, the developer in Las Vegas for whom you work doesn't design houses. He manages you. That's why he hired you.

If you advise on how to drive innovation in consumer product companies, the head of innovation who is your client doesn't design innovation strategies, she manages you. It's why she hired you.

Increasingly, our clients are like movie producers, an enduring metaphor that author Tom Peters originally gave us. Their jobs are to bring together the money, the story idea, the director, the cinematographer, the on-screen talent, the money, the studio's approval, the scriptwriter, the composer, the money, the editor, the production designer, the art director, and (did we say this?) the money.

That's the way it is with our clients. They want to make something happen in their worlds. They frame the task in the context of their company's strategic plan, borrow a junior manager from accounting to serve as controller, hire outside help, marshal their team, and find a budget. Their job is to bring together all the moving pieces and orchestrate an outcome. When it works, progress has been wrought, and they are the heroes.

And that is your invitation: You play an essential role in the collaborative ecosystem that drives progress across organizations. You bring a unique set of previous experiences, hard-won insight, and domain expertise to the table that, when combined with a host of other resources, can produce movie magic. It is exciting to be part of a team that really effects change. It is why, if you do a good job, you are often asked to return like Tom Hanks to a Stephen Spielberg production.

But know this: your expertise will sit alone, shipwrecked and starving on a distant desert island, your toes digging despondently in the sharp coral sand, unless you stand up and start calling attention to the work you do, the problems you are committed to solving, the conversation you want to underwrite, and the clients you most want to serve.

That is how experts connect with those they can most help.

Notes and References

Chapter 1   A Curious Problem

Dominic Barton quote: Interview with *How Clients Buy* research team, 2017.
Chuck McDonald quote: Interview with *How Clients Buy* research team, 2017.

Chapter 2   Finders, Minders, and Grinders: The Business Development Imperative

Russell Davis story: Interview with *How Clients Buy* research team, 2017.
The Cravath System story: Robert T. Swaine, *The Cravath Firm and Its Predecessors 1819–1948*, The Lawbook Exchange, Ltd. (originally published 1946).

Chapter 3   Beyond Pixels: Selling a Service Is Much Different from Selling Things (and Harder, too)

Credence Goods background: Asher Wolinsky, "Competition in Markets for Credence Goods," *Journal of Institutional and Theoretical Economics* 151 (1995): 117–31.
David Maister quote: Excerpt from his online article "Matters of Trust," 1998. http://davidmaister.com/articles/a-matter-of-trust/

Chapter 4 Obstacle #1—What They Didn't Teach You in B-School: If I Am Supposed to Be the Expert, Why Do I Feel So Stupid about Sales?

Thomas Jefferson story: "Notes for the Biography of George Wythe," Lipscomb, Andrew A. and Albert E. Bergh, eds. *The Writings of Thomas Jefferson.* Washington, D.C.: Thomas Jefferson Memorial Association of the United States, 1903–04. 20 vols., 1:166–70.

Walter Friedman quote: Walter Friedman, *Birth of a Salesman: The Transformation of Selling in America* (Cambridge, MA: Harvard University Press, 2005).

Ford Harding quote: Ford Harding, *Rain Making*, 2nd ed. (Avon, MA: Adams Media, 2008).

Richard Rosett quote: Richard N. Rosett, "Selected Paper No. 59, Business Education in the United States," Graduate School of Business, The University of Chicago.

Chapter 5 Obstacle #2—But I Don't Want to Sell: Moving Past Willy Loman

The Chuck Alpine story: Inspired by a real entrepreneur Tom McMakin heard speak during his private equity work.

Brian Jacobsen quote: Interview with *How Clients Buy* research team, 2017.

Audrey Cramer quote: Interview with *How Clients Buy* research team, 2017.

The Marvin Bower story: Elizabeth Haas Edersheim, *McKinsey's Marvin Bower* (Hoboken, NJ: Wiley, 2006).

The Hawkers and Walkers story: Friedman, *Birth of a Salesman*.

Chapter 6 Obstacle #3—Things Aren't What They Once Were: It Is Harder Than Ever to Sell Expert Services

The *Bates v. State Bar of Arizona* story: Thomas D. Morgan, *Gilbert Law Summaries on Legal Ethics*, 8th ed. (West Academic, 2005).

Mike Schultz quote: Mike Schultz, John E. Doerr, and Lee W. Frederiksen, *Professional Services Marketing*, 2nd ed. (Hoboken, NJ: John Wiley, 2013).

Warren Wittreich quote: Warren J. Wittreich, "How to Buy/Sell Professional Services," *Harvard Business Review*, March/April 1966.

Chapter 7   Obstacle #4—A Blizzard of Bad Advice: Everything You Know about Sales Is Wrong

Glengarry Glen Ross quote: *Glengarry Glen Ross*, 1992 American film, adapted by David Mamet from his 1984 Pulitzer Prize- and Tony-winning play of the same name, spoken by the character Blake, played by actor Alec Baldwin.

Fig. 7.01. The association of the sales funnel model was first proposed in *Bond Salesmanship* by William W. Townsend in 1924.

Chapter 8   The Secret to Selling: Never Say Sell

Walt Shill quote: Interview with *How Clients Buy* research team, 2017.

The Mac Shields story: Inspired by an actual client dialogue with Doug Fletcher. Names have been changed.

The Marvin Bower story: Edersheim, *McKinsey's Marvin Bower*.

The Design Thinking story: Tim Brown, "Design Thinking," *Harvard Business Review*, June 2008; Herbert Simon, *The Sciences of the Artificial* (Cambridge, MA: MIT Press, 1969); and Jon Kolko, *Design Thinking Comes of Age*, *Harvard Business Review*, September 2015.

The Arthur Chung story: Interview with *How Clients Buy* research team, 2017.

Chapter 9   Element 1—I Am Aware of You: What Was the Name of Your Firm Again?

The Dominic Barton story: Interview with *How Clients Buy* research team, 2017, and Dominic Barton, "The Teacher Who Inspired Me: Miss Stubson," *Huffington Post*, September 27, 2012, updated November 27, 2012, https://www.huffingtonpost.com/dominic-barton/the-teacher-who-inspired-_2_b_1917118.html

Ed Keller quote: Interview with *How Clients Buy* research team, 2017.

Stephanie Cole story: Interview with *How Clients Buy* research team, 2017.

Chapter 10   Element 2—I Understand What You Do: You Do What?

Mike Schultz quote: Schultz, Doerr, and Frederiksen, *Professional Services Marketing*.

The Cicero story: H. J. Haskell, *This Was Cicero* (Fawcett Publications, 1964).

Jack Trout quote: Jack Trout and Al Ries, *Positioning: The Battle for Your Mind* (New York: McGraw-Hill, 1981).

Patrick Pitman quote: Interview with *How Clients Buy* research team, 2017.

Kris Klein quote: Interview with *How Clients Buy* research team, 2017.

Jackie Kruger quote: Interview with *How Clients Buy* research team, 2017.

Ed Keller quote: Interview with *How Clients Buy* research team, 2017.

Dave Bayless quote: Interview with *How Clients Buy* research team, 2017.

Greg Engel quote: Interview with *How Clients Buy* research team, 2017.

Chapter 11   Element 3—I Am Interested: These Are My Goals

Chuck Walker quote: Interview with *How Clients Buy* research team, 2017.

Jimmy Rose quote: Interview with *How Clients Buy* research team, 2017.

Jack Bannister quote: Interview with *How Clients Buy* research team, 2017.

Chapter 12   Element 4—I Respect Your Work: You Have the Right Stuff to Help Me

Billy Newsome quote: Interview with *How Clients Buy* research team, 2017.

The Francesco Sforza story: Henry S. Lucas, *The Renaissance and the Reformation* (New York: Harper Bros., 1960).

Paul Bloom quote: Paul Bloom, "Effective Marketing for Professional Services," *Harvard Business Review*, September 1984.

Graham Anthony quote: Interview with *How Clients Buy* research team, 2017.

The Carlie Breen story: Interview with *How Clients Buy* research team, 2017.

Ford Harding quote: Harding, *Rain Making*.

Don Scales quote: Interview with *How Clients Buy* research team, 2017.

Chapter 13   Element 5—I Trust You: You Have My Best Interests at Heart

The Iraq War story: Dr. Leonard Wong, "Understanding Why Soldiers Decide to Fight," *The Balance*, September 2016. Reprinted with permission from the U.S. Army Strategic Studies Institute and U.S. Army War College Press, U.S. Army War College, Carlisle, PA.

The Trust story: Devon Johnson and Kent Grayson, "Cognitive and Affective Trust in Service Relationships," Johnson, Devon and Kent Grayson, *Journal of Business Research* 58 (2005): 500–07.

Morgen Witzel quote: Morgen Witzel, *Management Consultancy* (New York: Routledge Publishing, 2015).

Don Scales quote: Interview with *How Clients Buy* research team, 2017.

Peter Bryant quote: Interview with *How Clients Buy* research team, 2017.

Harry Wallace quote: Interview with *How Clients Buy* research team, 2017.

Jeff Denneen quote: Interview with *How Clients Buy* research team, 2017

Sarah Arnot quote: Interview with *How Clients Buy* research team, 2017.

Jason Wright quote: Interview with *How Clients Buy* research team, 2017.

Dave Smith quote: Interview with *How Clients Buy* research team, 2017.

Chapter 14   Element 6—I Am Able: I've Got Budget and Buy-In

Art Gensler quote: Arthur Gensler with Michael Lindenmeyer, *Art's Principles* (Wilson Lafferty Publishing, 2015).

Walt Shill quote: Interview with *How Clients Buy* research team, 2017.

Troy Waugh quote: Troy Waugh, *101 Marketing Strategies for Accounting, Law, Consulting, and Professional Services* (Hoboken, NJ: John Wiley, 2014).

Chapter 15   Element 7—I Am Ready: The Timing Is Right

Seth Godin quote: Seth Godin, "Permission Marketing," *Fast Company*, March 31, 1998.

Mike Schultz quote: Schultz, Doerr, and Frederiksen, *Professional Services Marketing*.

Troy Waugh quote: Waugh, *101 Marketing Strategies*.

Daryl Connor quote: Daryl Connor, *Managing at The Speed of Change* (New York: Random House, 1993).

Chapter 16 A Chain Is as Strong as Its Weakest Link: Using the Seven Elements as a Diagnostic Tool

Story about Bread: Heinrich Eduard Jacob, *Six Thousand Years of Bread: Its Holy and Unholy History* (New York: Lyons & Burford Publishers, 1997).

For Further Reading on MECE (Mutually Exclusive, Completely Exhaustive): Arnaud Chevallier, *Strategic Thinking in Complex Problem Solving* (New York: Oxford University Press, 2016).

Chapter 17 Getting to Work: Learning to Think and Act Like a Rainmaker

David Maister quote: David Maister, "Young Professionals: Cultivate the Habits of Friendship." (2005) http://davidmaister.com/articles/young-professionals-cultivate-the-habits-of-friendship/.

Sarah Arnot quote: Interview with *How Clients Buy* research team, 2017.

Tony Castellanos quote: Interview with *How Clients Buy* research team, 2017.

The Chuck McDonald story: Interview with *How Clients Buy* research team, 2017.

Arthur Chung quote: Interview with *How Clients Buy* research team, 2017.

Ed Keller quote: Interview with *How Clients Buy* research team, 2017.

Frans Cornelius quote: Interview with *How Clients Buy* research team, 2017.

Dr. Nate Bennett quote: Interview with *How Clients Buy* research team, 2017.

Peter Bryant quote: Interview with *How Clients Buy* research team, 2017.

Dominic Barton quote: Interview with *How Clients Buy* research team, 2017.

Don Scales quote: Interview with *How Clients Buy* research team, 2017.

The Cliff Farrah story: Interview with *How Clients Buy* research team, 2017.

Jane Pierce quote: Interview with *How Clients Buy* research team, 2017.

For Further Reading on the 1958 McGraw-Hill Ad: "Best Business-to-Business Ad of the 20th Century," *Advertising Age*'s *Business Marketing Magazine*, 1999.

Walt Shill quote: Interview with *How Clients Buy* research team, 2017.

Michael Hinshaw quote: Interview with *How Clients Buy* research team, 2017.

Chapter 18   All Business Is Local: From the Silk Road to the Information Superhighway

The Grand Bazaar story: Halil Inalcik with Donald Quataert, *An Economic and Social History of the Ottoman Empire, 1300–1914* (Cambridge: Cambridge University Press, 1994).

Story on AECOM: AECOM, Form 10-K, Annual Report, 2016.

Story on Nexsen Pruet law firm: Company history and geographic locations, http://www.nexsenpruet.com/

Chapter 19   Our Vision of the Future: A Roadmap for Change

Fig. 19.1. The Hedgehog Concept is from Jim Collins, *Good to Great* (New York: HarperCollins, 2001).

The Story about the Cold War: Melvyn P. Leffler and Odd Arne Westad, *The Cambridge History of the Cold War* (Cambridge: Cambridge University Press, 2010).

Mihaly Csikszentmihalyi quote: Mihaly Csikszentmihalyi, *Flow: The Psychology of Optimal Experience* (New York: Harper Perennial, 2008).

Acknowledgments

We would like to thank our families for their unwavering support during the writing of this book. We owe a sincere debt of gratitude for your understanding during the late nights and long weekends of this project. We also want to thank Rockford and Cold Smoke Coffee in Bozeman, Montana, for letting us hash out our ideas in their warm confines and write in their comfortable chairs for hours on end.

We'd like to individually thank the talented attorneys, consultants, accountants, architects, and finance professionals who shared their business development stories with us during the research of the book. Your insights and wisdom transformed this book from a dry business text into a lively narrative rich with plots and characters: Arthur Chung, Dave Smith, Jimmy Rose, Russell Davis, Cliff Farrah, Peter Bryant, Frans Cornelius, Audrey Cramer, Walt Shill, Nate Bennett, Jack Bannister, Don Scales, Dominic Barton, Michael Hinshaw, Paul Boulanger, Ashish Singh, Jason Wright, Ed Keller, Jane Pierce, Joshua Vesely, Jackie Kruger, Sarah Arnot, Jeff Denneen, Brian Jacobsen, Greg Engel, Dave Bayless, Tony Castellanos, Megan Armstrong, Billy Newsome, Graham Anthony, Chuck McDonald, Kris Klein, Patrick Pitman, Ann Kieffaber, and Chuck Walker.

We're grateful for our agent, Sheree Bykofsky, for seeing a glimmer of potential in our book idea. Without her, this book would never have gotten further than idle talk around a pub table. We'd like to thank the amazing team at John Wiley & Sons for making this book a reality, specifically Richard Narramore, senior editor of business publications, whose guidance in shaping this book was invaluable, and Danielle Serpica and Emily Paul for keeping this book on schedule and shaping it into a finished work. And finally, to Deborah Schindlar whose close attention to text gave our words polish.

We'd like to thank our main reader, Erin Strickland, for her helpful edits, her understanding of the Queen's English and, in particular, for her insights into the millennial generation.

Tom would like to thank the entire crew at PIE, without whom this book wouldn't have been written; Harry Wallace, for his vision that business development doesn't have to be about manipulating people but can rather be a form of high service; Jacob Parks, Matt Ulrich, Andi Baldwin, Emily LeVeaux, and Paul Quigley for your help with interviews; Andi Baldwin for her close reading and comments on the manuscript; John Nord, Jacob Parks, Matt Ulrich, and Stephanie Cole for giving him time to write the book as PIE's management team; Kristin Horgan, Carlie Auger, Cavin Segil, Susie Krueger, Andy Weas, Morgan Klaas, Renee Storm, Susan Miller, Melinda Murphy, Sophie Kevany, Alanna Rhinard, Windy Esperti, Renee Storm, Tanya Reinhardt, Josh Iverson, and Julia Yanker for their warm support; and finally, to Ann Kieffaber for her help in the Seven Elements diagnostic and Dave Bayless for his friendship, enthusiasm for all things business, a close read of a rough draft, and invaluable insight into the dynamics of trust.

Doug would like to thank Cliff Farrah, president of The Beacon Group, for his inspiration and friendship over the past twenty-five years. When Doug needs an honest opinion on something, he knows Cliff's candor and warmth is always a phone call away. Also, Doug thanks Cliff for introducing him to David

Maister. Not only did David's books shape Doug's understanding of what it means to be a trusted advisor, but David's support of North Star Consulting Group in its early days gave Doug's firm a chance to prove its worth on a global stage.

Doug is also thankful for his first boss in management consulting, Don Scales, for believing in him when he was green and lacked much to offer. Doug carried Don's briefcase through airports and rental car lots for two years after business school in exchange for a career's worth of knowledge on serving clients.

Doug would also like to thank the amazing professors that taught him at the University of Virginia's Darden School of Business and at Clemson University. These formational years led to a lifetime of relationships and memories.

Lastly, Doug would like to thank his cofounders at North Star Consulting Group, Dr. Mike Reilly and Eric Gregg. He is proud of the work they did together. He learned more from them than they'll ever know.

About the Authors

TOM McMAKIN is the CEO of Profitable Ideas Exchange (PIE), a leading consultancy focused on helping professional services firms with business development by building peer communities of likely buyers, and in training those who deliver professional services in how to grow their practices. Tom is the author of *Bread and Butter*, in which he described his work at Great Harvest Bread Co., and how he and his team created a nationally recognized corporate learning community and culture of best practices using collaborative networks. Before joining PIE, Tom was a cofounder and Managing Director with Orchard Holdings Group, a private equity firm as well as an Operating Affiliate at McCown DeLeeuw and TSG Consumer. He served for a decade as the chief operating officer of Great Harvest Bread Co., a multi-unit operator of bread stores. Tom is a graduate of Oberlin College and a returned Peace Corps Volunteer, having served in Cameroon, Africa. He and his family live in Bozeman, Montana.

Tom can be reached at tmcmakin@profitableideas.com.

DOUG FLETCHER currently splits his time between teaching at Montana State University's Jake Jabs College of Business & Entrepreneurship, and speaking/writing/coaching on the topic of business development in professional services and consulting. Additionally, he serves on the Board of Directors of The Beacon Group, a growth strategy consulting firm headquartered in Portland, Maine. Prior to that, he was cofounder and CEO of North Star Consulting Group, a technology-enabled consulting firm that specialized in global web-survey projects. North Star led the research that was the foundation on which the leading voice on professional services, David Maister, wrote his widely acclaimed book, *Practice What You Preach*. Earlier in his professional life, Doug served as a consultant with the management consultancy, A. T. Kearney, and was trained at General Electric in its leadership development program. He is a graduate of Clemson University and has an MBA from the University of Virginia's Darden School of Business Administration. Doug has called Bozeman, MT home for the past 20 years where he enjoys alpine skiing, mountain biking, and fly fishing with his friends and family.

Doug may be reached at doug@fletcherandcompany.net.

Index